Heavenly love

Heavenly love

The Song of Songs
simply explained

Gary Brady

EVANGELICAL PRESS

EVANGELICAL PRESS
Faverdale North, Darlington, DL3 0PH, England

e-mail: sales@evangelicalpress.org

Evangelical Press USA
P. O. Box 825, Webster, New York 14580, USA

e-mail: usa.sales@evangelicalpress.org

web: http://www.evangelicalpress.org

First published 2006

British Library Cataloguing in Publication Data available

ISBN-13 978-0-85234-606-8   ISBN 0-85234-606-9

Printed and bound in Great Britain by Creative Print & Design Wales, Ebbw Vale

This is dedicated to the one I love
i Eleri
f'anwylyd, fy ngholomen, fy mhriodferch, fy chwaer

Contents

		Page
Preface		9
Acknowledgements		12
1.	Clarifications: A basic introduction (1:1)	15
2.	Craving: What people rightly want and why (1:2-4)	27
3.	Courtship: Self-perceptions and desires — getting it right (1:5-8)	48
4.	Commitment: Models of care, devotion and fellowship (1:9 – 2:2)	64
5.	Coming together: The nature of true love (2:3-17)	80
6.	Crisis: A lover lost, a lover sought, a lover found (3:1-5)	104
7.	Ceremony: Two lovers married — a wedding procession (3:6-11)	119
8.	Consummation: Praising, wooing and loving (4:1 – 5:1)	134
9.	Coldness: The loss of close covenant communion (5:2-8)	160

10. Captivation: True beauty and where it is found
    (5:9 – 6:12)   177
11. Completeness: The nature of true love in its
    maturity (6:13 – 8:4)   201
12. Continuing: How to continue, commence and
    complete a loving covenant relationship
    (8:5-15)   223

Appendix   247
Select bibliography   255

Preface

Jewish rabbis used to warn against reading the Song of Songs before the age of thirty. Similarly, when recommending Bible books for his friend Paula's daughter to read, Jerome kept the Song until last. If you read it for yourself, especially in a modern version, you will see why. It is the reason why Dorothy L. Sayers' character Lord Peter Wimsey says that as a youth he 'got to know the Song of Songs pretty well by heart'.

Should there be a parental advisory sticker on commentaries on the book — especially ones that, like this one, take the view that the book is, at least in part, about marital love? Writing to the Ephesians, Paul certainly warns believers that there must not be even a hint of sexual immorality among them. Perhaps we tend to think of that as a prohibition against thinking about sex at all. In fact, of course, it means that we must keep all our thinking and speaking pure. Rather than hindering us from doing so, this commentary, like the book itself, is intended to help us to do just that, whatever our age or situation.

One former seminary president opined that in most situations the Song 'would probably not minister effectively to the entire congregation'. This commentary nevertheless grew out of a series of sermons preached to a congregation covering an ample range of both ages and experiences. The ideas preached at that time have been developed, but I trust that the commentary is characterized by the same sensitivity and appropriateness that I sought in the light of the variety of people present at that time.

Every good commentary should help us to relate to the Lord Jesus more intimately. That is what this one sets out to do. This is another area where we are often found wanting, and one where the Song can be of particular help to us. I trust that a perusal of this commentary will once again aid us in that respect. When newly converted, the great Jonathan Edwards spent a lot of time with the Song because it spoke to him so much of Christ's 'loveliness and beauty'. How gratifying if this commentary were to prompt a similar reaction in the life of some Christian, especially a recent convert!

For most of us, the areas of sexuality and spirituality are ones where we instinctively resist close scrutiny. I confess that living with this book over the period of writing this commentary has not been easy for that reason. It is my prayer that the insights that have hopefully been gained into these areas will, by the grace of God, be a blessing to those who study these issues for themselves.

In closing I want to say a few things about the commentary that may help you to get more from it.

Firstly, there is probably no book of the Bible about which there is more room for disagreement. Even if you agree with the general approach adopted in this volume, you may struggle with specific details of interpretation. Where that is so, I hope that you will seek to benefit from what insights there may be here, even though they may run counter to your own particular understanding of the passage.

Secondly, I do not intentionally take an allegorical or typical approach to the Song of Songs, but you may feel that at certain points I do. If I am guilty of faulty hermeneutics, I can only plead for clemency and ask that at least an eagerness to honour Christ and to see his lovely features in every place should be considered a virtue, not a fault.

Despite what has been said above, you may find some phrases that you consider indelicate, injudicious or unhelpful. I ask that you try to ignore these and hasten on. My only aim has been to help God's people, not to put a stumbling block before them.

As in a previous commentary in this series, my aim has been to be 'interactive', devotional, practical and Christian. I have relied largely on the NIV text but have consulted other texts.

Gary Brady,
Childs Hill,
January 2006

Acknowledgements

I was first introduced to the Song of Solomon as a boy in Pontrhydyrun Baptist Church in South Wales. My minister at the time, Derek Garwood, belonged very firmly to the 'spiritualizing' school and usually followed the method of tackling isolated texts of which Spurgeon was one of the best-known exponents. I gained a great deal from his ministry in general and some first helps in coming to grasp this particular part of the Bible.

During my university years in Aberystwyth I sat under the ministry of Geoff Thomas, who later became my father-in-law. I have particularly fond memories of his expository series on the Song of Songs. Geoff took a decidedly horizontal view of the book. It was also in this period that the complete NIV was first published. It sets out the Song in quite a helpful and striking way, and was a great aid to my understanding at the time.

My theological studies were undertaken chiefly at the London Theological Seminary, where I was further able to develop my understanding of the book through the lectures of a third Welshman, the current principal, Philip Eveson.

Over the years since that time, I have read many commentaries and other works, entered into various discussions and heard a number of addresses, all of which have served in one way or another to sharpen my appreciation for, and shape my understanding of, the book.

In 2002 I preached a sermon series to the congregation that I have happily served since 1983, at Childs Hill Baptist Church, London. Those sermons form the basis of the present book. The congregation's enthusiasm and occasional comments have been greatly appreciated.

I am indebted to Gary Benfold, pastor of Moordown Baptist Church, Bournemouth, for helpful comments on drafts of early chapters. Speaking one sunny Monday to a ministers' fraternal in Bedford was a great stimulus too.

The staff at Evangelical Press have again been kind and helpful. Comments from the original readers, even when reluctantly rejected, proved a great help in thinking the exposition through. It is a privilege to have such input.

I am again grateful to my father-in-law and to the Evangelical Library, London, for the loan of relevant books, also to the Library at LTS. Thank you to Darby Gray of Kidsdon for use of his verses in chapter 12.

Various aspects of computer technology were again harnessed for the execution of this assignment — the resources of the World Wide Web, Larry Pierce's *On-line Bible*, various *Ages Software* CDs and the whole *Word for Windows* word-processing package. Various technical problems seemed to dog me early on, but there were no major crises, for which I am thankful. Music from the Windows Media Player has only been occasional on this project. The Song of Solomon has a music of its own.

At the time of writing there was a rare flurry of engagements and marriages of folk connected to the Childs Hill fellowship. May these chapters be a help and blessing to you and other young couples.

My indebtedness to all my friends and family is vast. My wife, Eleri, is well aware how far short I fall of the ideals, both vertical and horizontal, which are set out here, but she is my Shulammite. *Diolch yn fawr f'anwylyd, fy nghariad!* You have stolen my heart, my sister, my bride; you have stolen my heart with one glance of your eyes, with one jewel of your necklace. How delightful is your love, my sister, my bride! How much more pleasing is your love than wine, and the fragrance of your perfume than any spice!

1.
Clarifications: A basic introduction

Please read Song of Songs 1:1

'In all the world there is nothing to equal the day on which the Song of Songs was given to Israel, for all the Scriptures are holy, but the Song of Songs is the Holy of Holies.'

Even allowing for hyperbole, Rabbi Aqiba's second-century statement contrasts sharply with the attitude of some Christians today, who apparently have little place for this book in their thinking or practice. They hardly ever quote it, read it or reflect on it. It has suffered what a modern writer calls 'functional decanonization'.

Such extremes remind us that the book has sometimes been controversial. Over the years, there have been both Jewish and Christian observers who have questioned its place in Scripture. From ancient times until the present day, however, I hasten to add, its divine inspiration has never been in any serious or lasting doubt.

Its location in Scripture

In Hebrew Bibles, the Song is the fourth book (after Psalms, Proverbs and Job) in the third and final main section, the

Sacred Writings. This diverse collection is mostly found between 1 Chronicles and the Song of Songs in English Bibles. Five books (the Song, Ruth, Ecclesiastes, Esther and Lamentations) are traditionally referred to as the *Megilloth* or scrolls. Modest, apparently insignificant works, they are given prominence at Jewish festivals, with the Song being read at the end of Passover.

Following the Greek translation known as the Septuagint, English Bibles place the book after Ecclesiastes. Some like that order, saying that Ecclesiastes does a negative, preparatory, convicting work ('Everyone who drinks this water will be thirsty again', John 4:13) while the Song is more positive, complete and edifying ('… but whoever drinks the water I give him will never thirst', John 4:14). These two, with Job, Proverbs and certain psalms, are often spoken of as Wisdom Literature, a genre dealing chiefly with how to apply truth to daily life. Duane Garrett says that its wisdom is obvious. It prepares the reader 'for the joy as well as the trauma of love'.

Like other Wisdom Literature, the Song is poetry. It uses terse sentences and devices such as parallelism (developing ideas through near repetition), assonance and alliteration (repeating consonants or vowels), simile or metaphor (rhetorical picture language) and refrain. As with most poetry, especially love poetry, the writing is highly imaginative and artistic ('perhaps the largest concentration of imagery anywhere in the Bible' according to Tremper Longman III). These factors can make for difficulties in interpretation.

Critical interpretation of the Song

More than one scholar has called the Song of Songs the most difficult book to interpret in the Old Testament. Augustine found it a puzzle. Tenth-century rabbi Saadia ben Joseph spoke of the key to its locks being lost. Matthew Henry said,

'It seems as hard as any scripture to be made a "savour of life unto life".' In 1683 a gentleman called Richard Coore issued a book expounding 'the most difficult texts' in Scripture. It included work on 'the two mystical books of canticles and the revelations'. A modern preacher speaks candidly of 'much furious thought and casting about in my mind to make something of' it, and another of being 'stark-raving bonkers' to take it on. Misgivings about its place in Scripture have sprung chiefly from wrestling with these problems.

A key question to consider before we begin, then, is the correct hermeneutical approach. At one extreme are those who want to take it in an entirely *spiritual* way. It deals exclusively, they say, with the love between God and his people. At the other extreme are those who want to take it in an entirely *natural* way. For them, it is all about the love between a woman and her lover, and no more. Across this spectrum there are several schools of thought. Some of these are outlined in the appendix.

In his *Introduction to the Old Testament*, Professor E. J. Young cites Church Father Theodore of Mopsuestia as one who took the Song literally. This led him to reject it from the canon, for which he was condemned in A.D. 533 at Constantinople. (In 1544 Calvin condemned Sebastian Castillio for a development of this same view. Castillio claimed the book was 'lascivious and obscene'.) Without condoning such radicalism, Young agrees with this broad approach. It reminds us, he says, 'in particularly beautiful fashion, how pure and noble true love is'. Like others, he then wants to extend the application beyond the purity of human love to include something higher, seeing here not an allegory, or even a type of Christ and his church, but a subject with a higher meaning.

The various interpretations probably all shed some light on the book. Without necessarily using Young's word 'parable' to denote the view, it is basically his approach that

I adopt in this commentary. It cuts the Gordian knot and is the approach that in my opinion provides the best interpretative framework. I believe that, when he wrote, the author had in mind both a natural and a spiritual understanding, and that those who originally received it as Scripture understood it both in terms of human love and intimacy and as a portrait of the loving relationship between God and his people.

Raewynne Whiteley puts it like this: 'Song of Songs could be understood as a superb love poem, evocative and rich in imagery. As such it sets forth a high standard for mutual love and encourages the celebration of love and beauty. However, as we understand the further dimension of God's love, it becomes an intimate invitation into relationship with God, celebrating the goodness of love, the beauty of passion and the tenderness of God.'

But on what basis do we take this view? When we look at Proverbs, another book closely connected with Solomon, we find references to the women Wisdom and Folly and to the wiles of the adulteress. It is commonly accepted that such references teach us both about fidelity in marriage and in God's covenant with his people. In a similar way, the Song works on two levels. Passages such as Psalm 45; Isaiah 62:4-5; Hosea 1-3 and Malachi 2:14 seem to do the same.

When Paul speaks to husbands and wives in Ephesians 5:22-25, we recall how he immediately moves to the subject of Christ and his church: 'Wives, submit to your husbands as to the Lord. For the husband is the head of the wife as Christ is the head of the church, his body, of which he is the Saviour. Now as the church submits to Christ, so also wives should submit to their husbands in everything. Husbands, love your wives, just as Christ loved the church and gave himself up for her to make her holy...'

He adds, 'This is a profound mystery — but I am talking about Christ and the church. However, each one of you also must love his wife as he loves himself, and the wife must respect her husband' (Eph. 5:32-33).

Here is a clue to the full understanding of the Song. It speaks not only about the important matter of human love between a man and his bride, but also the mysterious intimacy that exists, and that is to be cultivated, between true believers and their Lord and Saviour, Christ. Surely it is the sort of thing that we find in the Song that Paul has in mind when he writes, for example, 'I am jealous for you with a godly jealousy. I promised you to one husband, to Christ, so that I might present you as a pure virgin to him' (2 Cor. 11:2).

Other New Testament Scriptures that may relate back to the Song are references to Christ as the Bridegroom (Matt. 9:15; Luke 5:35; John 3:29; Rev. 19:7; 21:9; 22:17).

Contemporary application of the Song

In our own day a study of this ancient book is crucially needed in both these areas.

Firstly, because in this modern world of mass media, through advertising, cinema, television and the World Wide Web, we are inundated with false images of love, sex and marriage. We are bombarded with misleading ideas and, even if we keep our minds as pure as we ought, it is still very easy for inaccurate concepts to worm their way in and have their debilitating effect on us. In 2003 *Being Human*, a report by the Church of England's Doctrine Commission, spoke of 'saturation of virtually all channels of communication by sexual imagery of an increasingly explicit kind'. All of us — virgins or not, single, married, divorced or widowed, celibate or sexually active, young or old, male or female — need to be crystal clear on this vital subject.

Then, secondly, there is the vital issue of intimacy with Jesus Christ. Someone may be reading this who is not a believer. One of the purposes of this commentary is to help you to see how lovely the Lord Jesus is, how attractive, how appealing. I want you to fall for him and fall before him. As for believers, I truly hope that this book will help revive and rekindle our first love for him, where such a renaissance is needed. The aim is for us to see again something of Christ's beauty and glory, his comeliness and splendour, and so to be drawn to him. The Song of Songs can be of tremendous help to us in this direction.

The title of the Song

The book's title, or superscription, as found in our Bibles, is 'Solomon's Song of Songs'. This catchy title reflects something of the poetry of the original Hebrew. How old the details on this 'title page' are we do not know for sure. However, it seems to be authentic. It tells us three things.

1. Solomon

This is a book by or about Solomon, or at least it has something to do with him. Is it simply dedicated to him, or in his style, or one that was his favourite? It is difficult to be totally sure who the author was, but there is no reason to reject out of hand the tradition that it was Solomon. Also called Jedidiah, 'beloved of the LORD' (2 Sam. 12:25), Solomon has sometimes been regarded as an Old Testament parallel to the apostle John. Some see the references to him within the book as peripheral, but his name is mentioned seven times (1:1,5; 3:7,9,11; 8:11,12). There are also references to 'the king' (1:4,12; 7:5). The book seems to come from a time when Israel was peaceful and united. Note references to

Jerusalem, Carmel, Hermon, etc. It is worth remembering that in Hebrew the name Solomon is similar to the word *Shalom*, peace, as is Shulammite (the term used to refer to the woman in 6:13). At the start of the book the idea of peace and fulfilment is in the background.

There is something attractive about the ancient Jewish view that the Song of Songs, Proverbs and Ecclesiastes are the works, respectively, of Solomon's earlier, middle and later years. Henry Morris is one modern writer who takes this view. He argues that here Solomon has in mind his first love and bride, Naamah, an Ammonitess, mother of Rehoboam (2 Chr. 12:13), whom Solomon must have married in his late teens. Morris backs up this speculation by noting the reference to Engedi (1:14), just across the Dead Sea from Ammon, and the use of the word 'pleasant', possibly a diminutive of Naamah, in 1:16. The fact that Solomon later went astray in the very area of human and divine intimacy, with his many wives and his idolatrous ways, does not of itself undermine the book's value. Indeed, this factor acts as a warning sign discouraging the idea that there is any easy way to escape such temptations.

If we accept that Solomon is the author, the book dates from somewhere in the middle of the tenth century B.C. Many who deny this view, on linguistic or other grounds, want to give it a much later date.

2. Song

It is a song — here a pleasant and joyful thing, as songs usually are, 'to stir up the affections and to heat them', as Matthew Henry puts it. It is poetry, which is good for stirring the emotions but can also be useful for didactic ends. We all know what it is to have the words of a song in our heads — whether we want it there or not. In English, the book is sometimes known as 'The Song' and sometimes, slightly inaccurately, as 'Canticles' (from the Latin Vulgate's *Canticum Canticorum,* The Song of Songs).

3. Song of songs

'Song of songs' could mean a song made up of different songs, a collection, a 'best of' compilation even. Although one song, it has various parts. However, the phrase probably means 'the best of songs' and is similar to biblical phrases such as 'vanity of vanities', 'King of kings' and 'Holy of holies' (hence the penchant for this term for the Song among older writers). The Aramaic Targum says that out of ten songs, including those of Moses, Deborah and Hannah, this is Scripture's ninth and best song. We learn that Solomon 'spoke three thousand proverbs and his songs numbered a thousand and five' (1 Kings 4:32). Here we have the very best of them, the most beautiful. Nick Hornby has written of popular music that 'In the end it's songs about love that endure the best.' This is certainly a song about love. It is not only Solomon's best song but inspired Scripture, and so doubly worthy of careful and diligent study. It also has, as has been suggested above, the greatest theme of all — Jesus Christ, the one who is love personified. Puritan James Durham says it deals with the best subject (Christ and his church), in its most glorious aspect (their mutual love), is an excellent composition with a captivating style, and comprehensively provides 'an armoury and storehouse of songs' suitable 'for every case' and 'for all sorts of believers'.

An outline of its construction

Some see the Song as a collection rather than as a single literary unit, identifying as few as six, or as many as over thirty, different poems here. Others argue for a greater unity.

The Song may lack the plot one expects from a story, but it forms a coherent totality that is the result of more than merely assembling an anthology. However the Song was put together, there is a definite cohesion, with the same characters, recurrent phrases and ideas, and similar language throughout.

Some writers reject the idea of linear development through the book but, while there is no consensus on details, there is some agreement on the broad narrative structure. The order is: first, a courtship period, which probably includes formal betrothal (1:1 – 3:5); second, the wedding (3:6 – 5:1); and third, married life (5:2 – 8:14). S. Craig Glickman states that all commentators accept that 'the wedding procession' (3:6-11) forms a unit. He believes that the lovemaking sections (4:1 – 5:1; 7:1-10), are almost as clear-cut. As 4:1 – 5:1 follows the wedding procession, has the beloved being addressed for the first time as a bride and sees her wearing a veil, it is reasonable to understand it as a wedding-night scene.

The section 7:1-10 has its corollary in 7:11 – 8:3. The section that links 3:6 – 5:1 and 7:1 – 8:3 is 5:2 – 6:13. This is a 'conflict and solution narrative' that can be seen as bridging the gap between the lovemaking of 4:1 – 5:1 and its more intense parallel in 7:1-10. That leaves the opening and closing sections, 1:1 – 3:5 and 8:4-14. The first of these is probably a courtship section rather than a flashback, the only such scene occurring near the end of the book, where the climax and resolution appear. The courtship can be split after 2:3, where there is increased intensity. Glickman thus ends up with seven or eight sections: 1:1 – 2:3; 2:4 – 3:5; 3:6-11; 4:1 – 5:1; 5:2 – 6:13; 7:1 – 8:4; 8:5-14 (or 8:5-9; 8:10-14).

Some writers are uneasy about the idea that the pair marry before the end. Those who take a 'spiritual' view rightly point out that the relationship between Christ and his church is most often seen in terms of betrothal here on earth and marriage in the world to come. However, back in the seventeenth century, Puritan Edward Pearse wrote of there being a threefold marriage between Christ and his people. He denotes these as personal, mystical and heavenly.

By 'personal' he means Christ 'the Word made flesh', what theologians call the hypostatic union. This is foundational. By 'mystical' he means 'being joined to the Lord and being one spirit with him'. This is our initial participation in Christ. By 'heavenly' he means the glorious union in heaven, the consummation to come. This involves full possession and enjoyment for ever. Here in the Song of Songs it is this 'mystical' marriage that is in mind.

Because of these and other issues, different writers have different outlines for the contents of the Song. In this book we shall use the following plan:

1:1	Clarifications: A basic introduction
1:2-4	Craving: What people rightly want and why
1:5-8	Courtship: Self-perceptions and desires — getting it right
1:9 – 2:2	Commitment: Models of care, devotion and fellowship
2:3-17	Coming together: The nature of true love
3:1-5	Crisis: A lover lost, a lover sought, a lover found
3:6-11	Ceremony: Two lovers married — a wedding procession
4:1 – 5:1	Consummation: Praising, wooing and loving
5:2-8	Coldness: The loss of close covenant communion
5:9 – 6:12	Captivation: True beauty and where is it found
6:13 – 8:4	Completeness: The nature of true love in its maturity

8:5-14   Continuing: How to continue, commence and complete a loving covenant relationship

As has already been stated, some deny that events are presented in a largely sequential way. Others posit many dream sequences, flashbacks and reminiscences. Some do this from a quite proper concern to avoid suggesting any pre-marital sexual encounters in the book. There is, however, no need to resort to such devices in order to maintain this position.

We should also note that the Song is constructed with two main characters and a sort of chorus.

1. The beloved — the woman, the 'beloved' (NIV), the Shulammite

She appears to be a young country girl, possibly from Shunem in Lower Galilee (see 6:13), possibly Naamah the Ammonitess. She is betrothed to her lover and marries him. For over half the time she is the one who speaks (fifty-five out of 117 verses). She is an active initiator. She corresponds to the woman in betrothal and marriage and to God's people in 'spiritual' terms.

2. The lover — the man, King Solomon, her 'lover' (NIV)

His speeches take up just under forty per cent of the book. He exemplifies the role of the man in a male-female relation-ship and illustrates Christ's love for his people.

3. The friends

From time to time we also have comments from 'the friends, the daughters of Jerusalem'. Their contribution is small, just over five per cent, although they also act as an audience at some points, a sort of sounding board for the woman's ideas. Who exactly they are is disputed. Are they ladies-in-waiting at Solomon's court, friends of the woman, or general onlookers? They act as observers and serve to draw the woman out.

The nature of Hebrew is such that, although there is sometimes a doubt, it is usually clear whether a male or a female, a single person or more than one, is speaking.

There is something here, then, not only for men and for women on the matter of courtship, love and marriage, but also for all who look on and see such things happening.

A summary of the narrative

It is useful, finally, to have an idea of the storyline that, I believe, underlies the unfolding of the book. Perhaps 'storyline' is too strong a term — this is a song, not a novel or a play. Despite the denials of some, however, a plot is detectable. We can debate details, but it seems that the beloved was part of a family where the father had died, or was no longer on the scene for some other reason, and where she was under the authority of her half-brothers. Naturally beautiful, she was a somewhat neglected soul, forced by her guardians to work long hours under a hot sun in the vineyards and in other agricultural pursuits.

One day a handsome stranger appears and shows interest in her. This man, it turns out, is King Solomon. He sees her hidden beauty, wins her heart, betroths her to him, marries her and takes her into his palace. Although there comes a time when she takes his love for granted, and so drives him away, they are reconciled and come to a mature love that goes on into the future with no sign of ending.

2.
Craving: What people rightly want and why

Please read Song of Songs 1:2-4

Mark and Sarah are Christians, both in their early twenties. They like each other a lot and want to be more intimate. Neither has been a Christian for very long and neither is entirely sure how to approach this matter. They have many questions. Are such strong sexual feelings permissible? How far can these be expressed before marriage? What is the difference between legitimate desire and illegitimate lust?

Other Christians in the same church who know Mark and Sarah well have noticed their growing friendship. Some are unsure what to say to them, if anything, or how to help things along.

Meanwhile, the pastor of the church has been lacing recent sermons with searching questions about people's relationship with Christ. How close is it? How real? Why are we often slow to express our love for Christ in the presence of others?

Can you identify with any of the characters in this scenario? What we find here in the opening verses of the Song will help us in these areas.

In 1:1-8 the woman appears to be the chief speaker. Up to the start of 1:4 she speaks of her lover. The friends then comment, it seems, in the rest of 1:4. From there through to 1:7, she speaks about herself and her lover, and another comment from the friends probably follows in 1:8. Here we consider 1:1-4.

The probable circumstances are debated. Are these teenagers, a couple on their wedding day, or an older couple reminiscing? Is this a king and his princess, a shepherd and his country lover? The verses, I would suggest, describe the first love between Solomon and his beloved. The focus is on a time before any marriage between the two. Some sort of prehistory is assumed.

Elizabeth Huwiler observes the ambiguity here — unintroduced and unidentified speakers and hearers, undefined circumstances, ambivalent images, etc. The urgency and uncertainty demand our involvement and 'aptly [express] the riotous flow of emotions in the young lovers'. The pattern appears to be as follows:

Shulammite	Friends	Solomon
1:2-4a	—	—
—	1:4b	—

These verses teach us about our approach to love between men and women and illustrate something about our approach to fellowship with the Lord Jesus Christ, the King greater than Solomon.

What do they want?

Twentieth-century film director Sam Goldwyn once suggested that for a successful film you need to start with an earthquake and then work up to a climax! The Song works on similar lines. Longman says that the opening 'sets a dynamic tone that never ends throughout the book'.

Travel back in your mind to the year 1914. Imagine the people of the quiet, conservative town of Lewes, Sussex, on England's south coast, and the shock it was to them when they discovered what was on show at the town hall. It was a marble version of Auguste Rodin's famous statue of Dante's Paulo and Francesca, *The kiss*! They were taken aback. What a scandal! Many protested at the disgrace. The virtual bombshell that landed then is not dissimilar to the one that explodes in the abrupt and passionate opening here, as the beloved blurts out, **'Let him kiss me with the kisses of his mouth'** (1:2).

There is an intensity about the Hebrew; hence the NEB's 'Let him smother me with kisses.' She is so intoxicated with him that she does not even use his name. Her thoughts are full of *him* — who else could *he* be?

Kissing does not lack variety. There are kisses of honour, peace, friendship and affection. This kiss has passion, a passion that does not exclude purity. There are kisses on forehead, cheeks, hands, feet, the ground a person treads. This is a kiss on the mouth. There are kisses from superiors, inferiors or equals. Here it is a kiss from the king himself that she craves.

In 1:4 the woman also says to the king, **'Take me away with you — let us hurry! Let the king bring me into his chambers.'** She not only wants him to come to her, but she also wants to go to him. The Hebrew actually says, 'The king has brought me...', but the context suggests a wish rather than its fulfilment.

Today, in the Western world, lovers can be seen kissing in public. In the East, this is very unusual. In recent years, in fact, more than one Eastern country has talked of outlawing such public displays of affection. She wants them to be in private, therefore, in his chambers, so that they may share intimacies.

Lips have twenty times as many touch receptors as, say, the legs, and throughout the world a kiss on the mouth is seen as a passionate, intimate act. Much has been written on the subject. Such a kiss, most agree, should be both ardent and affectionate. Nineteenth-century author Christian Nestell Bovee said, helpfully, that 'the passion that is in a kiss' is what gives it its sweetness and 'the affection in a kiss ... sanctifies it'.

This type of kiss has been called 'the very autograph of love'. It has a unique nature and symbolism, since it is something that you cannot give without taking, nor take without giving. Actress Ingrid Bergman once spoke of it as 'a lovely trick designed by nature to stop speech when words become superfluous'. This 'rosy dot placed on the "i" in loving', as someone else put it, is 'a secret told to the mouth instead of to the ear'. The German writer Emil Ludwig was probably right when he observed that 'The decision to kiss for the first time is the most crucial in any love story. It changes the relationship of two people much more strongly than even the final surrender; because this kiss already has within it that surrender.'

There are three things to note in the biblical text.

1. The woman rightly craves intimacy with the man

She has the feeling that 'I want to be with you, be with you night and day.' Men and women have various emotions or longings. In God's eyes, these can be right or wrong. Wrong desires or cravings are often perversions of right ones. For example, without putting these in the same category as sexual desire, the inclination to eat or drink is good and necessary. The desire to be a glutton or to be drunk is neither good nor necessary.

Here we discover that what the woman wants is intimacy with the man. She yearns to be with him, to be near him. She wants to be alone with him. A kiss on the mouth is a most intimate sign of that sort of friendship, and this is what she craves. The 'king's chambers' are his own private rooms, not a public part of his palace. She wants to be with him there.

She is not condemned for these desires, as they are perfectly right and proper in their own place. It is only when they are perverted that there is a problem. There is a difference between what we may best term 'desire' and lust. Humanists, and even Roman Catholics, are unclear about this but, just as we can distinguish between legitimate and good sexual activity and unlawful, sinful sexual activity, so we can differentiate between legitimate and illegitimate sexual desire.

I recently received publicity from a Christian organization publicizing a conference on the growing problem of addiction to internet pornography. Interestingly they entitle their presentation 'Searching for intimacy'. That is exactly what most people who get caught up in such things are doing. The desire for intimacy is fine. The way that some are going about it is a major problem.

Creation scientist Henry Morris says, 'The marvellous phenomena of sexual love and reproduction, with the amazing complex of mechanisms involved, could never have originated by some random evolutionary process. God created it all, and He has, in effect, reminded us of its grandeur by including this beautiful Song of Solomon in His divinely inspired Scriptures.'

Back in Genesis 2:21-25 we read of how God caused Adam 'to fall into a deep sleep' and took part of his side to make 'a woman from the rib he had taken out of the man'. He then 'brought her to the man', who declared her to be 'bone of my bones and flesh of my flesh' and called her 'woman'. Led by the Spirit, Moses comments, 'For this reason a man will leave his father and mother and be united to his wife, and they will become one flesh.'

At that time, 'The man and his wife were both naked, and they felt no shame.' However, with the advent of sin, the relationship between man and woman was affected so that pure and holy desires were perverted and corrupted. The woman, who is under the spotlight in Genesis 3:16, is told, 'Your desire will be for your husband, and he will rule over you.' The idea is of the natural order continuing, but with certain distortions.

Men and women have legitimate cravings for intimacy. The way that God has made us is such that we normally enjoy the proximity of others and interaction with them. We desire friendship and company, intimacy and emotional closeness and a sexual relationship with another person. There have been Christians who have frowned on some of these ideas, or have simply tried to pretend that such feelings do not exist. This is neither right nor wise.

The 2003 Church of England Doctrine Commission's report *Being Human* even suggested that the permissive society is possibly 'one of the long-term consequences of the failure of Christians to maintain a positive Christian view of sexuality as a gift of God in creation'.

The tradition among the early and medieval fathers was pretty much against all sexual desire, even within marriage. As Oscar Wilde's Canon Chasuble put it, 'The precept as well as the practice of the Primitive Church was distinctly against matrimony' (prompting the droll response: 'That is obviously the reason why the Primitive Church has not lasted up to the present day'!).

With the dawn of the Reformation and a return to a biblical understanding of creation, things changed. Heiko Oberman has written of how 'Luther wanted to liberate the Christian faith from this distortion'. 'Whoever is ashamed of marriage', wrote Luther, 'is ashamed of being human.' According to Leland Ryken, the seventeenth-century Puritans believed that 'it was God who had created people as sexual beings'. As a modern writer put it, 'The first sexual thought in the universe was God's, not man's.' Ryken also says that the Puritans rightly saw sex as a 'natural or biological appetite'. Harry Stout says, 'They were not prudes... For husband and wife sex was important, and Puritan families were routinely large. A spouse could be punished by the authorities for withholding sex from his or her partner.'

Surely this is a right and biblical attitude. We have these longings and, although they are often perverted and become sinful, where the desire is for my spouse or, if single, for one particular unmarried person of the opposite sex, they are not in themselves wrong. Desire must not be confused with love, of course, but it is perfectly compatible with it. Paul says to the unmarried and widowed that 'It is good for them to stay unmarried, as I am,' but is equally clear that 'It is better to marry than to burn with passion' (1 Cor. 7:8,9). Passion is acceptable but it is like fire — fine under control, but potentially dangerous if not approached with care.

Writing of the love of her Puritan husband, Colonel John Hutchinson, his wife Lucy declared, 'Never was there a passion more ardent and less idolatrous. He loved her better than his life.' The American Puritan poet Edward Taylor described his own desire for his beloved as like 'a golden ball of pure fire'. That sums it up well.

William Smith, a Presbyterian minister in Alabama, is bold enough to say that 'You cannot read the Song of Solomon and believe that love does not involve hot emotions, physical desire and rich romance.' When interviewing couples wishing to marry, he speaks not only of the need to be ready to sustain a lifelong commitment to each other but also asks first, 'Do you love each other with Song of Solomon love?'

Most people want to have someone to be alone with, someone to talk to, to share with, to be intimate with. Sometimes such passions are legitimately fulfilled, at least for a period, in this life. Sometimes they are not. For a single person to want to fulfil those yearnings, or for a married person legitimately to gratify those cravings in the marriage bed, is not sinful (see 1 Cor. 7:3-5). It is both natural and right.

2. The woman rightly wants the man to take the lead

It is perhaps worth remarking that, although the woman seems to be the one making all the moves, she does not simply want intimacy with the man, but she wants him to take the lead in this. We have already noted how central her role is in the book. She is certainly no shrinking violet here. Rather she is something of an initiator. For some writers this is a problem. In the 1950s one commented that such initiative from a woman is 'never the case in secular love'. Would he write like that today? Whether he is right or not, it is important to note that she wants *him* to kiss *her*, not for her to kiss him. She wants him to be the instigator. She wants *him* to take *her* away, not for her to take him away. She wants *him* to take *her* to his chambers, not for her to take him to hers, or to meet in some neutral place.

This is how it should be, biblically. There is such a thing as male headship in the Bible, and it is reflected here. Often under attack from unbelievers, and sometimes from believers too, it is plainly taught in Scripture. Right desires will fall into line with this fundamental pattern, not in a way that demeans women as citizens, but in one that, while leaving plenty of room for female initiative and ingenuity, exhibits willing submission to male headship in the marriage bond. There is a beautiful reciprocity in biblical courtship and marriage. The woman invites; the man responds. The man instigates; the woman accepts. When this reciprocity is misunderstood and it is assumed either that women are to lead, or that they can do nothing to invite love, the biblical norm is lost sight of.

When we are children, our needs for intimacy are met, or ought to be met, chiefly by our parents or by those *in loco parentis*. They kiss us, keep us, care for us and do all sorts of other things for us. Our duty is to honour and obey them. As we grow older, our appetite for intimacy with someone outside our family grows to varying degrees. Such yearnings are lawful and are to be met through marriage and all that leads up to it.

It is right for a man to want a woman with whom he can be intimate and for a woman to want a man to bring about this intimacy. Marriage can last a short time or a long time — a lifetime in many cases, at least on one side. No marriage is perfect, but provided that the man takes the lead and that the wife is submissive, according to biblical patterns, then one thing that it can do very well is to meet our emotional need for intimacy here on earth. For various reasons some stay unmarried and so those desires remain, and must remain, largely unfulfilled on a physical level. To have those cravings is nevertheless right and legitimate, understandable and unobjectionable.

3. The one we should all desire — Jesus Christ

Always in Scripture we should seek to see how it points us to the Lord Jesus. Christ himself says of the Scriptures that they 'testify about me' (John 5:39). As in England all roads lead to London, so in the Bible all roads lead to Christ. Jesus, we must not forget, was fully human and in the first place we here gain an insight into the desires he must have known yet chose to deny for the sake of the kingdom. Further, it is surely fair to say, in the light of these verses, that whatever our situation, it is always right and proper, indeed absolutely vital, to desire intimacy with the Lord Jesus Christ. We were made for God — to be with him and to serve him. We should, as it were, covet the kisses of his mouth. We should yearn to be alone with him, face to face. We should long, in Richard Sibbes' words, 'that he would reveal himself every-day more and more'. If you truly know him, you will want that.

Professor Eugene Peterson likes to tell the story of a woman coming to him for help. Having attended a number of counselling sessions, she expected him to discuss her sex life, and was surprised that he wanted instead to talk about her prayer life. The two matters are closely connected, he says. Both are about intimacy. He asserts that a deep hori-zontal relationship will involve aspects of sexuality and a profound vertical one will involve prayer. The two intercon-nect. A secular American women's magazine discovered this, to its surprise, when a survey on sexual satisfaction suggested that the more religious a woman was, the more likely she was to be sexually fulfilled.

If we follow Emil Ludwig's cue, quoted above, we can say that any real longing for the consummation of love in heaven above will translate to a desire for God's kisses here below. Think of Peter's words: 'Though you have not seen him, you love him; and even though you do not see him now, you believe in him and are filled with an inexpressible and glorious joy' (1 Peter 1:8).

What is it that holds you back from intimacy with Christ? Why do you not want to draw nearer to him? Are you ashamed of him in some way? Is it that you are simply taken up with other things?

Some people never marry and are sorry about it. Perhaps they have loved and lost, or maybe they have never loved at all in that way. One understands their possible regret. Some marry and, for various sad reasons beyond their control, the marriage may soon be over. To lose out on such intimacies is a loss, but a brief and passing one in the light of eternity. Far,

far more heart-rending is the tragedy of missing out on a relationship with Jesus Christ. Nothing can possibly make up for missing out on that. It is a disaster of infinite and eternal proportions. Nothing can compare to intimacy with him. If you have never put your faith in Jesus Christ, do you realize this? If you are a believer, are you keeping in mind how precious intimacy with him is? The kiss of homage and devotion must be given:

> Kiss the Son, lest he be angry
> and you be destroyed in your way,
> for his wrath can flare up in a moment.
> Blessed are all who take refuge in him
>
> (Ps. 2:12).

Can we say with David, 'How lovely is your dwelling-place, O LORD Almighty!'? Do our souls yearn, faint even, 'for the courts of the LORD'? Can we say, 'My heart and my flesh cry out for the living God'? (Ps. 84:1,2).

If we have tasted and seen that the Lord is good, surely we should have what Sibbes calls 'an insatiable desire for a further taste and assurance of his love'. Isn't this the nature of true love? When we consider the infinite riches of Christ, we know that we can only have scratched the surface so far. We should labour for a clearer sight of the Lord. This involves turning from all false teaching and laying aside every worldly distraction. Samuel Rutherford once wrote to Lady Kenmure in these terms: 'I trust ye are so betrothed in marriage to the true Christ, that you will not give your love to any false Christ.' With humility and zeal we must build on what we already have so that, slowly but surely, as we prayerfully serve him and know his comfort in our sorrows, we increasingly feel a sense of his sweetness and love.

Pray, 'Take me away with you' — literally, it is, 'Draw me.' God says, 'I have loved you with an everlasting love; I have drawn you with loving kindness' (Jer. 31:3; see Hosea 11:4; John 12:32). 'The Lord Jesus Christ', says Richard Brooks, 'is the magnet of redeemed souls.' Pray for greater attraction, for further drawings: 'Draw me nearer, nearer, nearer, blessed Lord, to thy precious, bleeding side.'

Be earnest about this. He draws us to himself, but we must run towards him. Say to your heart, 'Let us hurry!' Do not hang back for a moment. With Eliza Hewitt say:

More about Jesus would I know...
More of his saving fulness see,
More of his love who died for me.

Pray that the King will 'bring me into his chambers'. Pray in song:

Love divine, all loves excelling,
Joy of heaven to earth come down!
Fix in us thy humble dwelling.

May the love of Jesus fill me
As the waters fill the sea.

O Jesus Christ, grow thou in me
And all things else recede.

Thee will I love,
My Strength, my Tower...
Thee will I love, till the pure fire
Fills my whole soul with strong desire.

Say with Augustus Toplady:

Compared with Christ, in all beside
No comeliness I see;

The one thing needful, dearest Lord,
Is to be one with thee.

The sense of thy expiring love
Into my soul convey;
Thyself bestow, for thee alone,
My all in all, I pray.

Loved of God, for him again
With love intense I'd burn;
Chosen of thee ere time began,
I choose thee in return.

Why do they want it?

The second thing to note here is *why* people rightly long for such things.

1. Why the woman craves intimacy with the man

The woman answers the question as to why she craves intimacy with the man at the end of 1:2 and in 1:3 (assuming she is the speaker throughout 1:2-4. The switch from 'him' to 'you' may sound strange but often occurs. It is called *enallage*). Why does she yearn for intimacy with him?

> **… for your love is more delightful than wine.**
> **Pleasing is the fragrance of your perfumes;**
> > **your name is like perfume poured out.**
> > **No wonder the maidens love you!**

'**Delightful**' and '**pleasing**' translate the same Hebrew word. The words form a pattern:

For *pleasant* is your love, more than wine.
The fragrance of your perfumes, *pleasant* it is.

The word for **'love'** here is not the usual Hebrew word
and may denote lovemaking rather than love as an emotion.

For her, there is nothing to compare with his lovemaking,
or with his caresses! Later she says, 'His mouth is sweetness
itself; he is altogether lovely' (5:16). Here she compares
receiving his kisses to drinking wine, a powerful metaphor
that appears several times in the book (1:4; 2:4; 4:10; 5:1;
7:9; 8:2) and a common one in the ancient Near East. There
is a play on the similarity of the two Hebrew words used and
the fact that wine flowing over the lips, like a kiss on the lips,
can produce a delightful sensation and more. There is delight
in the bouquet of a glass of wine, or in drinking it, or in a
similar experience, for that matter. To know love and intimacy is even more delightful. Perhaps the intoxicating power
of wine is in the background too. Love can make a person
giddy or light-headed.

Having spoken of touch (kisses) and taste (wine), she then
talks about his beautiful aroma. This may seem a little odd.
Is she saying that she is drawn to him by the smell of his
aftershave? (See also 1:13-14; 3:6; 5:13). In a hot climate
and in the days before modern plumbing, lotions and perfumes were particularly important. In Hebrew, the words for
'perfume' and **'name'** are again similar. She uses this as a
picture of what his name, or his character, is like. Ecclesiastes 7:1 uses a similar image: 'A good name is better than fine
perfume.'

John Owen comments: 'As the smell of aromatical spices
and flowers pleases the natural sense, refreshes the spirits,
and delights the person; so do the graces of Christ to his
saints. They please their spiritual sense, they refresh their
drooping spirits, and give delight to their souls.' He notes

that their hearts are ravished in particular by the 'precious perfume of his death'.

She does not simply like the way this man looks; everything about his character draws her to him. Nor is this only her opinion. The maidens, virgins of marriageable age, all admire him too. **'How right they are to adore you!'** says the beloved (1:4).

Glickman makes the application that a young girl today should be able to speak in a similar way of the man she hopes to marry. She should not be the only one who sees what a great catch he is, either. She should not be so infatuated that she takes a fool for a genius, thinks Quasimodo is Prince Charming, or mistakes a rogue for a knight in shining armour.

She, then, on one hand, must be looking for the right sort of man. Young men, on the other hand, ought to seek to be men of good character — not spineless or weak, but upright, honest, holy, devout, worthy of respect and entitled to a woman's love and esteem.

2. Why we should all seek intimacy with Jesus Christ

As to why we should seek intimacy with Christ, the answer is surely obvious. There is none to compare with him, no one who even begins to match him! He has the name that is above every name, the name high over all.

Blessed are those who have learned to acclaim you,
  who walk in the light of your presence, O LORD.
They rejoice in your name all day long;
  they exult in your righteousness

(Ps. 89:15-16).

The Lord's name is his character, a character that is matchless. The delight of knowing his love is beyond compare. In John Newton's famous words:

How sweet the name of Jesus sounds
In a believer's ear!
It soothes his sorrows, heals his wounds
And drives away his fear.

Or as a later hymn puts it:

There is a name I love to hear,
I love to speak its worth;
It sounds like music in my ear,
The sweetest name on earth.

A lesser-known verse of that same hymn echoes the sentiments here:

This name shall shed its fragrance still
Along this thorny road,
Shall sweetly smooth the rugged hill
That leads me up to God.

Do you long for spiritual intimacy with Christ? Do you long to be alone with him? If you have any idea of his true worth you surely will. The 'kisses of his mouth' are for those who, by grace, see his worth, appreciate his significance and value his greatness. Can you say with Asaph, 'Whom have I in heaven but you? And earth has nothing I desire besides you'? (Ps. 73:25).

Various writers suggest aspects of Christ's love that make it superior to wine — it can be enjoyed without fear, brings eternal delight, totally satisfies, is supremely beneficial and is absolutely pure.

In 1872 C. H. Spurgeon spoke of Christ's love as better than wine. Negatively, it can be taken without question, costs nothing and never cloys. Drunks can put their wine away, as they are filled by its deadly draught, 'but never did he who drinks of the wine of Christ's love become satiated or even content with it; he ever desires more and yet more of it'. It is without impurities, never turns sour and causes no ill effects. Positively, it has certain healing properties, imparts strength, symbolizes joy and provides 'sacred exhilaration', the holy energy to serve.

For a Christian it is hard to read of wine and of the pouring out of oil or perfume without thinking of Jesus Christ and the Lord's Supper, with its wine poured out, which speaks so powerfully of his life's blood spilled on the cross to save sinners. Remember John's words: 'This is how God showed his love among us: He sent his one and only Son into the world that we might live through him. This is love: not that we loved God, but that he loved us and sent his Son as the one who would turn aside his wrath, taking away our sins' (1 John 4:9-10).

In the wedding psalm, the writer says of Christ:

You love righteousness and hate wickedness;
> therefore God, your God, has set you above your
> > companions
> by anointing you with the oil of joy.
All your robes are fragrant with myrrh and aloes and
> > cassia;
> from palaces adorned with ivory
> the music of the strings makes you glad

(Ps. 45:7-8).

Our response should be like that of the psalmist elsewhere:

Because your love is better than life,
   my lips will glorify you.
I will praise you as long as I live,
   and in your name I will lift up my hands.
My soul will be satisfied as with the richest of foods;
   with singing lips my mouth will praise you
                         (Ps. 63:3-5).

References to perfume also remind us of the way pure nard was poured out on Jesus in preparation for his burial and suggest the earlier pouring out of the Spirit on Christ at his baptism, especially when we remember the perfumed quality of sacred anointing oil in Old Testament ritual, symbolic of the Holy Spirit.

What should we think of such longings?

In the second part of 1:4 we have what seems to be a comment from the friends: **'We rejoice and delight in you; we will praise your love more than wine.'**

The phrase **'we will praise'** really means, 'we will remember in order to praise'. The friends are delighted at this love match. They are happy with the attitude of the man and the woman and they think that lovemaking itself is an excellent thing — better than wine, symbolic of joy and fellowship. We also should be glad when we see biblically contoured affection blossoming between two people. We want to encourage it, not hinder it because we are jealous, disdainful or indifferent.

Conversely, we shall want to discourage desires for intimacy that are not biblically based. This includes perversions such as fornication, adultery, homosexuality, paedophilia and the use of pornography. Some try to argue that such things are acceptable. There is nothing in this song, or anywhere else in the Bible, to support such views, and everything to oppose them. See for example, the following passages: 'The acts of the sinful nature are obvious: sexual immorality, impurity and debauchery...' (Gal. 5:19). 'See that no one is sexually immoral...' (Heb. 12:16). 'Put to death, therefore, whatever belongs to your earthly nature: sexual immorality, impurity, lust, evil desires and greed, which is idolatry. Because of these, the wrath of God is coming' (Col. 3:5-6).

Those who struggle with such temptations ought not to despair, however, for in Corinth people were converted, it is clear, who had been 'sexually immoral ... adulterers ... male prostitutes ... homosexual offenders' (1 Cor. 6:9-11). Many others have been redeemed from similar lives.

Further, we ought to be doing all we can to encourage one another in our love for Jesus Christ and in our devotion to him. He should be our joy and delight and whenever we meet someone who loves the Lord, we should be glad. We ought always to speak in the highest terms of what it means to be a Christian. There is nothing better than to know Jesus Christ. What a glorious thing it is! How marvellous! How wonderful! How magnificent! There is nothing greater. What are we doing to promote such things?

Another mention of wine here, especially in the context of remembering (AV, 'We will remember thy love more than wine') again causes believers to think of the Lord's Supper. Before evening communion on 2 November 1890, Spurgeon appropriately took this text and spoke of Christ's love — the fact of it, its character, its deeds and its proofs in experience.

To be a Christian, as has already been intimated, is to relish the character of Christ. It is to identify with words such as these, usually attributed to Bernard of Clairvaux:

Jesus, the very thought of thee
With sweetness fills the breast;

But sweeter far thy face to see,
And in thy presence rest.

Perhaps that verse is familiar. There are others:

No voice can sing, no heart can frame,
Nor can the memory find
A sweeter sound than thy blest name,
O Saviour of mankind!

O hope of every contrite heart,
O joy of all the meek,
To those who fall, how kind thou art!
How good to those who seek!

But what to those who find? Ah, this
Nor tongue nor pen can show;
The love of Jesus, what it is,
None but his loved ones know.

Another hymn says:

O Jesus, King most wonderful,
Thou Conqueror renowned,
Thou sweetness most ineffable
In whom all joys are found!

When once thou visitest the heart,
Then truth begins to shine,
Then earthly vanities depart,
Then kindles love divine.

To sum up

While we observe biblical norms, such as proper respect for male headship, to crave lawful sexual intimacy is right and good. Unmarried women should look for the right sort of man; unmarried men should seek to be men of good character, worthy of admiration and respect. Further, while we should all want to discourage unbiblical cravings for intimacy, we shall also want to encourage unattached believers to unite in marriage with others in the faith, as the Lord leads them.

All believers should long for greater intimacy with the Lord Jesus, the one whose name is above all names. He is pre-eminently attractive, the one we should all desire first and foremost. We should always want to encourage each other in our love for him and in our devotion to him.

3.
Courtship: Self-perceptions and desires — getting it right

Please read Song of Songs 1:5-8

Mark and Sarah, the couple we thought of in the last chapter, are facing other problems. As they contemplate a relationship together, they sometimes have to admit to qualms about their own attractiveness to each other. Both are sometimes plagued by self-doubt.

Several Christians in the same congregation are also having problems with self-perception. Although their pastor speaks often enough, not only of sin, but also of the love of God in Christ, they find it hard at times to believe that Christ has a genuine interest in them.

Once again, readers may be able to identify with this state of affairs. If so, there is help for us here. The pattern of speakers in this passage is as follows:

Shulammite	Friends	Solomon
1:5-7	—	—
—	1:8	—

We have already thought about right desires and the expression of them. Now we turn to the matter of the right way for people to think about themselves, and why; we also consider the right way lovingly to pursue one another and, once again, the role of onlookers in all this.

Self-perception

In 1:5 the woman is speaking to the daughters of Jerusalem. These are, presumably, relatively sophisticated women, as they live in the capital city, at the hub of the nation. As this country girl speaks about herself, it is clear that she is rather self-conscious in their presence. For the first time she expresses a little self-doubt and insecurity. She begins:

> **Dark am I, yet lovely,**
> **O daughters of Jerusalem,**
> **dark like the tents of Kedar,**
> **like the tent curtains of Solomon.**

Women's fashions change, as do opinions on what is attractive. At certain times in the nineteenth century, for example, the bustle was *de rigueur* for fashion-conscious young ladies. In the 1920s, a flat chest was felt to be essential for a woman. At one time long skirts and natural colours may be popular, but then it is the turn of shorter skirts and brighter colours. As I write, ponchos are back in vogue after a thirty-year break. Trends come; trends go.

There are cultural differences too. It has been noted how Western women often try to make their eyes look more like those of Eastern women, while oriental women frequently try to look more like their occidental counterparts. In some countries, 'Thin is in and stout is out,' while in others, 'Fat's where it's at' and 'No one's keen on lean'! While some African women are busy trying to lighten their skin colour with cosmetics, creams and drugs, their North European counterparts are under the sun lamp, or busy with fake tan, trying to achieve the opposite effect!

In Solomon's time, the desire was for a lightly coloured epidermis; indeed, the paler the better. Whatever shade of skin this woman was born with, it is certainly now darker than she would have liked. We shall see why in a moment. The first point to notice, however, is that she is wondering how someone as unattractive as she believes herself to be could possibly be of any interest to the great Solomon.

Having said all this, we notice a paradox. At the same time she says that she is **'lovely'**. Indeed, by referring to the black **'tents of Kedar'**, the goat-hide tents of the desert Bedouin tribes south-east of Damascus, darkened by their exposure to the elements, and to the **'tent curtains of Solomon'** (either those in his palace or, anachronistically, those of his temple — the new tabernacle) she may be suggesting the idea, not only of blackness on the outside, but also of treasure within. Alternatively, the rough 'tents of Kedar' may correspond to her darkness, and the well-crafted 'tent curtains of Solomon' (not Salma — an unhelpful emendation), which could be colourful, not dark, would refer to her loveliness. Isaac Watts took it that way:

Though in ourselves deformed we are,
And black as Kedar's tents appear,
Yet, when we put thy beauties on,
Fair as the courts of Solomon.

Her ambivalence is typical of adolescent self-perception and the attitudes of young lovers. In a more balanced way, it is also a theme in Scripture with regard first to the Messiah, then to the believer and his perceptions of himself. Isaiah says of the Christ:

> He grew up before him like a tender shoot,
>   and like a root out of dry ground.
> He had no beauty or majesty to attract us to him,
>   nothing in his appearance that we should desire him
> (Isa. 53:2).

And yet we know that ultimately he has everything to make us desire him. 'In Christ all the fulness of the Deity lives in bodily form' (Col. 2:9), and he has great 'glory, the glory of the One and Only, who came from the Father, full of grace and truth' (John 1:14).

As for believers, they are free from condemnation (Rom. 8:1), 'full of goodness' and 'complete in knowledge' (Rom. 15:14); the world is not worthy of them (Heb. 11:38), yet they are nothing in and of themselves. In Paul's words, 'Though outwardly we are wasting away, yet inwardly we are being renewed day by day. For our light and momentary troubles are achieving for us an eternal glory that far outweighs them all. So we fix our eyes not on what is seen, but on what is unseen. For what is seen is temporary, but what is unseen is eternal' (2 Cor. 4:16-18).

We have the 'treasure in jars of clay to show that this all-surpassing power is from God and not from us' (2 Cor. 4:7). We know that God 'gives strength to the weary and increases the power of the weak' (Isa. 40:29) and, though our heart and flesh fail, we can say with Asaph, 'God is the strength of my heart and my portion for ever' (Ps. 73:26). That is why we are to seek what Peter calls 'the unfading beauty of a gentle and quiet spirit, which is of great worth in God's sight' (1 Peter 3:4).

Also, think of the disjuncture between the unbelieving world's attitude to believers and the way that God sees us. Paul is fond of this contrast. He says of himself and other apostles, in words partly reminiscent of the beloved's own, 'To this very hour we go hungry and thirsty, we are in rags, we are brutally treated, we are homeless. We work hard with our own hands. When we are cursed, we bless; when we are persecuted, we endure it; when we are slandered, we answer kindly. Up to this moment we have become the scum of the earth, the refuse of the world' (1 Cor. 4:11-13).

Psalm 149:4 tells us that 'The LORD takes delight in his people; he crowns the humble with salvation.' Another relevant verse is 1 John 3:1: 'How great is the love the Father has lavished on us, that we should be called children of God! And that is what we are! The reason the world does not know us is that it did not know him.'

There is, then, a remarkable mixture of modesty and self-assurance in this woman. She knows that she is unworthy of Solomon, yet she also knows that he is attracted to her. That same fusion of humility and confidence ought to be with us in our relationships. As the saying goes, we all have a lot to be humble about. Even the best of us — what have we really achieved? There is certainly something very unattractive about boasting. On the other hand, if we are believers, we are aware that we all have God-given graces and talents, various assets with which the Lord has provided us.

The corollary is that we cannot reasonably expect perfection in others. A person may seem faultless to us at first, but we can be sure that there are insecurities and anxieties, spots and blemishes, imperfections and flaws, for us to regret and to cover over.

God has made men and women with cravings for intimacy, with sexual desire, and if you aspire to such things there is no reason why, if you are realistic, you should not find sexual intimacy with someone in Christ. More than that, God has made us for himself and, although we are sinful and unworthy, he nevertheless wants men and women like us, and boys and girls too, to come to Jesus Christ and to be intimately related to him.

It sounds crazy on the face of it, perhaps. Many mock the
idea: 'Why would King Solomon be interested in a poor
farm girl?' 'Why would the King of kings be interested in
someone like me? Why should he want to know me?' Yet
that is the plain teaching of Scripture. Human love is a great
thing. It is usually a wonderful feeling to know that someone
wants to marry you. 'Me? Why should he (or she) want to
spend his (or her) life with me?' Singer Paul Jones wrote
some words that many a man can identify with:

What does that woman see in me?
What does she see that I could be?
Why does that woman keep me 'round?
If I was her, I'd kick me out.

Even greater still is to know that Jesus wants me. And he
does. Do you know that? Do you realize how great his
desires for you are? Have you come to him yet? Have you
known his intimate embrace? His arms are open and out-
stretched in love towards all who will come to him. Come to
him today.

In 1894 W. Spencer Walton wrote the hymn 'In tenderness he sought me'. He pictures the Lord as the Good Sa-
maritan and includes the striking line: 'I wondered what he
saw in me, to suffer such deep agony.'

This is a thought we find commonly expressed by Christian writers. In 1962 an American Indian believer, Martin N.
Huaxcuatitla, wrote a hymn in Tetelcingo Aztec, which
translates as:

What did you see in me,
Beloved and blessed God?
I have nothing good to offer,
My Lord Jesus Christ.

Just before her death in 1863, Jane Crewdson wrote these
two poignant verses:

> O Saviour, I have naught to plead,
> In earth beneath or heaven above,
> But just my own exceeding need,
> And thy exceeding love.
>
> The need will soon be past and gone,
> Exceeding great, but quickly o'er;
> The love unbought is all thine own,
> And lasts for evermore.

Listen to Jesus' wooing words in Matthew 11:28-30:
'Come to me, all you who are weary and burdened, and I
will give you rest. Take my yoke upon you and learn from
me, for I am gentle and humble in heart, and you will find
rest for your souls. For my yoke is easy and my burden is
light.'

Self-nurture

The beloved goes on speaking to the friends. She says:

> **Do not stare at me because I am dark,**
> **because I am darkened by the sun.**
> **My mother's sons were angry with me**
> **and made me take care of the vineyards;**
> **my own vineyard I have neglected**
>
> (1:6).

Although a very minor difference genetically, the melanin
that colours our skin can be quite noticeable. Shades vary
from one ethnic grouping to another, and within ethnic

groups as well. We are all affected too, to a greater or lesser extent, by solar rays. Obviously in the days before a detailed knowledge of the sun's ultra-violet beams, before suntan lotions, creams and oils, with their various sun protection factors, those who did not have to go out into the fields and work — that is, the rich city folk — tended to have the lighter-coloured skin. Those who worked hard in the fields — the poor country folk — tended to have darker skin. The reason that this woman was **'dark'** (the word is found only here in the Old Testament) — not literally black like 'the tents of Kedar', but certainly darker than Solomon — was that she was disadvantaged and had had to work in the fields. This was a social matter, then, not a racial one.

She had been forced to do this, it transpires, to enrich her brothers, probably her half-brothers. (They are, literally, her 'mother's children'; no father is mentioned, here or elsewhere, so presumably he had died.) Here is male headship again, but this time of a perverted and predatory sort. We do not know why the brothers were angry with her. There is a play on their being hot with anger and their sending her out to work in the hot sun. She was very conscious of her swarthiness and of the way people stared at her whenever she was in town. It was embarrassing and awkward. It made her feel uncomfortable and ashamed.

The woman goes further. She has to confess that, although she has taken care of other vineyards, literally and metaphorically, **'My own vineyard I have neglected.'** This is not a reference to her being either promiscuous or prudish. Rather, it refers to what we may term her sex appeal. Her vineyard is her own appearance and person. A well-kept vineyard is something natural yet orderly. It is a useful metaphor for a woman's person (or a man's, for that matter). The need for self-cultivation is ever present.

Spurgeon, typically, once used the text to warn Christian workers against neglecting their hearts — 'Do you ever use

the hoe upon those weeds which are so plentiful in us all?'
— or their families (as in the case of a Sunday School
teacher who never prays with her own children) or the
'vineyard round about their own house': 'Poor stuff, poor
stuff, is that salt which is only salt when it is in the salt-box!'

The matter of self-image raises itself here again, then.
Physically, temperamentally, and in other ways, we are
limited as to what we can achieve. We must, on the one
hand, struggle to improve, and on the other, learn to accept
that certain things are the way they are. We need to try to
make progress while recognizing our own limitations.
Getting the balance is not always easy. Why are we as we
are? Because we are in a world that, although created
perfect by God, is a sinful, fallen world, where we sin and
are sinned against, where things are blemished and
blighted, defective and damaged, substandard and spoiled.
This leaves its mark. The various trials and tests that we
face can be discouraging at times. We are filled with shame
and disgrace. It is humiliating.

We were created in God's image, but that image is
twisted and marred. While taking sin seriously, we must not
become disheartened but must see that, although our blemishes make us ashamed, by God's grace we can be 'lovely'
in the eyes of Christ. He does not overlook sin, of course, but
he understands why we have the faults and flaws in us that
we do, and also where these are not of our own making. We
can be delivered from guilt and shame through him and what
he has done on the cross. The image of God in us can be
reconstituted through gazing into the face of Christ.

Preaching on Song of Songs 1:5-6, Richard Sibbes taught
that God's people are imperfect on earth (outwardly and
inwardly). God allows this in order to draw us from earth,
humble us and increase our patience. We must confess our
blackness to him and long for heaven, not being discouraged
but seeing our glory. Our sovereign Deliverer can help us as

he has helped his saints in the past. We must remain upright and refrain from fretting. We must be humble and learn to be encouraged. There is glory, in the midst of many defects and disgrace, in our new name, nature, fortune, family and Guide. How blind we are by nature, but what comfort is here! Let's not be like flies on a wound, or dogs among rubbish, over-emphasizing deficiencies. That is a defiant, unjust and thoroughly bad way to act.

We must take courage, then, and learn to go to God with the right mixture of modesty and assurance, lowliness and boldness, meekness and confidence, humility and daring. He 'crowns the humble with salvation' (Ps. 149:4). We can say confidently with David:

> Though my father and mother forsake me,
>   the LORD will receive me…
> I am still confident of this:
>   I will see the goodness of the LORD
>   in the land of the living
>
> (Ps. 27:10,13).

All we need do is:

> Wait for the LORD;
>   be strong and take heart
>   and wait for the LORD
>
> (Ps. 27:14).

Self-respect

In 1:7 the woman addresses the king and makes her request:

> **Tell me, you whom I love, where you graze your flock**

> **and where you rest your sheep at midday.**
> **Why should I be like a veiled woman**
> **beside the flocks of your friends?**

Whether Solomon was literally a shepherd, like his father, does not entirely matter. She is speaking of him in poetic and romantic terms. The words **'flock'** and **'sheep'** have been supplied by the translators. Here, as elsewhere, some commentators find a sexual *double entendre.* Such suggestions are notoriously difficult to assess. Revising this commentary I spotted an unintentional one in one of my own chapter headings. Some people can give anything a sexual connotation. The saying, 'It's not the mouth it comes out of but the mind it goes into,' is relevant. I, for one, deem it wisest not to be too eager to find such phenomena.

The woman wants to come and see him, and so she wants to know exactly where to find him. She wears a veil to hide her identity from others, but does not want people to think she is **'a veiled woman'**, which probably means a prostitute. Not all veiled women were prostitutes, but we remember how Tamar 'covered herself with a veil … at the entrance to Enaim, which is on the road to Timnah' when she took up that role (Gen. 38:14). If the beloved knows where her lover is she will not need to wander from field to field, possibly giving the impression that she is not respectable. She wants to be with her lover, but does not want to do anything to lose her good reputation in the process. She wants to see him in the right way and at the right time too — midday, not midnight. **'Midday'**, of course, is the hottest part of the day, quite oppressive in that part of the world, necessitating rest in the shade for the flock, which means that at this time the sheep would not be demanding the shepherd's full attention.

1. The character of the beloved

So we learn a little more of the woman's commendable character. She wants to be respectable. She wants to conduct herself demurely and in the proper way. How admirable! Whenever people pursue a relationship, it is important that they do so with the utmost propriety and decorum. There must be nothing sleazy or shady about it, nothing seedy or sordid. Young people should meet each other in public, in open places such as in church, around the family table, at a bowling alley, or somewhere similar. A parked car on a dimly lit street, or the gloom of a discotheque, or somewhere like that, is not a good place. The darkness of a cinema or a theatre is probably not the best place either, at least not unless they are in the company of a larger group. Further, women who are eager to be desired must be careful not to give the wrong impression. Great care must be taken, especially in our day and age, over the choice of clothing and the way they conduct themselves.

At the same time, it is important for young people and older singles to meet one another. Accessibility is an important factor in any relationship that is going forward. Couples who spend no time together are bound to have problems. Deliberately playing hard to get is not an acceptable strategy in courtship.

On the vertical level, it is equally true that time is necessary to build a relationship with the Lord. In the words of William Longstaff:

Take time to be holy, speak oft with thy Lord...

Take time to be holy, the world rushes on;
Spend much time in secret with Jesus alone.

There are no quick fixes or instant solutions. As in every other relationship, quality time is vital.

2. The character of the lover

We also learn something here about the lover's character. He is pictured as a shepherd, a favourite image for a leader in Scripture, especially of the Lord himself. It conjures up a picture of someone who is hard-working, yet tender and sympathetic. Here is one who cares for his flocks and fights off attacks from wild animals, and so will care for all those who come to him. Go to Jesus, the Good Shepherd, the Great Shepherd, the Chief Shepherd. He will watch over you and he will care for you. In an eighteenth-century baptismal hymn the West-Country preacher Benjamin Beddome taught us to pray:

> Dear Saviour, tell us where
> Thy sweetest pastures grow;
> Thither with haste would we advance,
> Where living waters flow.
>
> Direct us to thy flock;
> With them may we abide,
> Protected from the noonday beams,
> And resting near thy side.

Unselfishness

We note, finally, the words of 1:8:

> **If you do not know, most beautiful of women,**
>   **follow the tracks of the sheep**

and graze your young goats
   by the tents of the shepherds.

These could be the lover's words or someone else's. If they are the man's, he is probably being playful or teasing. We shall take them here as spoken by the friends. They want this woman to know where to find her shepherd lover. Notice, too, how complimentary they are. It could be sarcasm, of course, but it is more likely that they are sincere. It is certainly our job to encourage each other always.

They tell the woman where to look for her lover. It is obvious in some ways — he is with his sheep, of course. They are not so much informing her as encouraging her. As for her **'young goats'**, we remember how Jesus contrasts goats unfavourably with sheep (Matt. 25:31-46, drawing on Ezek. 34:17), but we must be wary of pushing the image too far.

So we ought to do what we can to encourage healthy, biblically shaped relationships between people, and do all in our powers to show them the way to the Lord Jesus. Where is he? He is found most often among his sheep. Wherever his people meet, he is in their midst, as he promised (Matt. 18:20). Where the other pastors or under-shepherds are, there he is. In other words, come and listen to the Word preached. You will not regret seeking Christ. Seek him earnestly. Ask him to teach you the meaning behind words like these, which, like those at the end of the last chapter, are attributed to Bernard of Clairvaux:

O Jesus, King most wonderful,
Thou Conqueror renowned,
Thou sweetness most ineffable
In whom all joys are found!

When once thou visitest the heart,
Then truth begins to shine,
Then earthly vanities depart,
Then kindles love divine.

Or again:

Jesus, may all confess thy name,
Thy wondrous love adore,
And, seeking thee, themselves inflame
To seek thee more and more.

Thee, Jesus, may our voices bless,
Thee may we love alone,
And ever in our lives express
The image of thine own.

O Jesus, thou the beauty art
Of angel worlds above;
Thy name is music to the heart,
Inflaming it with love.

To sum up

Our self-perception ought to be marked by both modesty and confidence. There is not only much about ourselves that we should be ashamed of, but there are also, by God's grace, things that may appeal to others. We should think of others similarly.

If you pursue a relationship it should be with great decorum. If you are eager to be desired, take care not to give the wrong idea. Remember, too, that such things take time and care. We must all do what we can unselfishly to promote healthy, biblical relationships.

We are sinners by nature, but God's love is such that Christ can set us free from sin. He understands why we are as we are and can deliver from guilt and shame through his atoning death. Go to the Great Shepherd who watches over and cares for all who turn to him. Spend quality time with him. Then do all you can to point people to Christ. Wherever his people meet, Christ is there. Sinners should be encouraged to come and hear his Word preached.

4.
Commitment: Models of care, devotion and fellowship

Please read Song of Songs 1:9 – 2:2

In recent years the media have had a lot to say about 'super-models'. This term refers to a select band of women who are paid large sums of money to tread Europe's catwalks wearing a variety of designer clothing, promoting houses of *haute couture* and their designers. In this next section of the Song of Songs we have a set of supermodels — not the sort you will find in a modern fashion show, but examples, or paradigms, for people like Mark and Sarah, their fellow believers and people like us.

'Model' can be defined in at least two ways. One of these is potentially unflattering: 'imitation of the real thing; a replica, an imitation or reproduction'. It can also be defined as 'a pattern for others to emulate, a prototype or paradigm'. This latter meaning is the one I have in mind. Here we are presented with models, with examples, or ideals, for our emulation and duplication, both on the horizontal, human plane and the vertical, Godward one.

Initially, in 1:9-11, the lover, the king, speaks for the first time about the woman, his beloved. He describes her in very positive terms. Then, in 1:12-14, she responds. She seems to be at the king's dining table. A banquet is in progress.

Perhaps this is the time of their formal betrothal. Maybe it is a less formal and more intimate occasion. Whichever it is, she has eyes only for him. Finally, in 1:15 – 2:2, we have a delightful series of brief exchanges between them. The arrangement, I would suggest, is as follows:

Shulammite	Friends	Solomon
—	—	1:9-11
1:12-14	—	—
—	—	1:15
1:16	—	—
—	—	1:17
2:1 (?)	—	(2:1?)
—	—	2:2

Here, then, are three models for us to consider.

A model of kingly care

We shall begin by observing the praise that the king heaps on his beloved and his promises to her, and then make some practical applications for ourselves.

1. Praises announced

'My darling', he calls her. It is a strong term, exclusive to this book. Always found on the lips of the king, it occurs here for the first of nine times. It has also been translated 'my love' or 'my dearest'. It carries the idea not only of caring for someone, but also of being delighted to do so. The king loves this woman. She is his beloved. His attitude to her is quite unlike that of her brothers.

'I liken you, my darling,' he says, **'to a mare harnessed to one of the chariots of Pharaoh'** (1:9). This could mean a horse pulling Pharaoh's chariot, or one bought from Pharaoh to pull Solomon's own chariot. However, we should note that the idea of being **'harnessed'** is implied rather than stated.

This seems an odd way to speak of a woman, perhaps, although the idea of sleekness is appropriate. Some men refer to women as 'fine fillies', and others make favourable comparisons with other animals, such as cats, dogs, lambs and deer. Henry VIII's reference to Anne of Cleves as the 'Flanders mare' was decidedly unflattering, but when Helen of Troy was compared to a horse it was much more complimentary. In 1969, Jacques Levy wrote the words for the Byrds' hit song, 'Chestnut mare'. Ostensibly about a horse, it is clearly in fact about a woman. Levy calls her 'the prettiest mare I've ever seen', declaring that he will 'catch that horse' if he can and give her his brand. 'And when I do,' he says, 'she'll be mine for life; she'll be just like my wife.'

What is the exact point of comparison here in the Song? What is it about Pharaoh's horses that the writer has in mind? Several possibilities have been suggested:

They were high-quality thoroughbreds.
They were very expensive to obtain or maintain.
They were of personal interest to the king.
They were the king's delight.
They were wild by nature, but had been tamed, as in
    the song about the chestnut mare.

Some commentators say, either that mares were not used to pull chariots, or that the lead horse was a mare. In other words, this points to the woman's uniqueness in his eyes.

Another proposal, supported by ancient texts, is that as only stallions pulled Egyptian chariots, enemies would send in mares on heat to drive them into an equine frenzy. So the woman drives him wild. She stirs strong sexual desires.

Most probably the point of comparison is the careful way in which such handsome horses were elaborately decked out with beautiful jewels, feathers, ornaments, coloured leathers and fabrics. This speaks of this girl's innate beauty, supplemented by finely crafted jewellery and other accessories. She is beautiful and dignified. As has already been intimated, this poor girl is conscious of how unworthy she is to come into court. She is lovely, yes, but 'dark like the tents of Kedar'. 'Do not stare at me,' she pleads, 'because I am dark, because I am darkened by the sun … my own vineyard I have neglected.' Here the king heartens her with compliments.

He continues by saying, first, **'Your cheeks are beautiful with earrings, your neck with strings of jewels'** (1:10). Then he adds, **'We will make you earrings of gold, studded with silver'** (1:11).

These remarks confirm the explanation put forward above for the simile involving the mare. There is even some ambiguity as to whether these words describe the woman or the horse! The word translated **'earrings'** may mean braided hair, bangles or nose rings, but the reference is clearly to some form of decoration or ornament. The thing about the adornments is the way they enhance her beauty. The Bible is often positive about women's adornment (e.g. Gen. 24:22; Ps. 45:12-13; Prov. 25:12; 31:22; Ezek. 16:10-14), but does urge caution (Isa. 3:16-24; 1 Tim. 2:9-10; 1 Peter 3:3-5).

2. Promises added

The **'we'** in **'We will make you earrings of gold, studded with silver'** could point to the friends, or the king with the friends. It could be a royal 'we' for some reason. However we understand it, the point is that the woman's limited resources are not going to be a problem — the king himself, along with whoever else he needs to co-opt, has supplied, and will supply, all the jewellery and ornamentation that this woman could ever need.

3. *Practical applications*

Firstly, on the human level, there are lessons for both men and women regarding courtship. In any relationship there can be a sense of inadequacy, at least on one side or the other. It is right for the stronger partner to assuage such feelings with words of encouragement and appropriate gifts. Lovers and husbands should assure their loved ones that they truly are loved and show it with both words and deeds. Women, on the other hand, ought to be willing to receive such assurances and such gifts gratefully, even, dare I say it, when they are perhaps not as well chosen as they might be.

Secondly, there are lessons for us on the heavenly level. Always with this song we want to look higher than the horizontal. Here we are surely justified in hearing these words as the words of Christ to his bride, the church, when he says:

> I liken you, my darling, to a mare
> harnessed to one of the chariots of Pharaoh.
> Your cheeks are beautiful with earrings,
> your neck with strings of jewels.
> We will make you earrings of gold,
> studded with silver.

Christ, the King, is enthralled by his church and gives her an abundance of good gifts to honour and beautify her and prepare her for the glories ahead. For the way that Christ certainly does deal with his people, see, for example, the words of Peter: 'His divine power has given us everything we need for life and godliness through our knowledge of him who called us by his own glory and goodness. Through these he has given us his very great and precious promises, so that through them you may participate in the divine nature and escape the corruption in the world caused by evil desires' (2 Peter 1:3-4).

We remember also Ephesians 5:27, which describes how Christ works 'to present her [his people] to himself as a radiant church, without stain or wrinkle or any other blemish, but holy and blameless'. If the precious blood of Christ has been spilt for us, will God withhold anything that we need? 'He who did not spare his own Son, but gave him up for us all — how will he not also, along with him, graciously give us all things?' (Rom. 8:32).

A model of submissive devotion

Next the beloved speaks again. As we have noted, she seems to be at the king's dining table. There is perhaps a betrothal feast going on, or possibly it is some more private occasion. Whatever the situation, she has eyes only for her lover. In response to his promises, she says:

> **While the king was at his table** [or possibly 'on his couch'],
> **my perfume spread its fragrance.**
> **My lover is to me a sachet of myrrh**
> **resting between my breasts.**
> **My lover is to me a cluster of henna blossoms**
> **from the vineyards of En Gedi**
>
> (1:12-14).

His 'my darling' is matched by her **'my lover'**, used here for the first of some thirty-one times. It is a term of affection and intimacy.

We move from visual images to olfactory ones. The power of her response is reinforced by her reference to no less than three different perfumes — the word translated **'perfume'** being literally 'nard', an expensive perfume from the Himalayas. This is the perfume with which Jesus was anointed at Bethany, you may remember. Matthew Henry draws a link between this passage and John 12, as Jesus, the King, was at his table then, too.

We usually associate **'myrrh'** with death, but it was used quite widely, in both solid and liquid forms. It was common in that culture for women to wear a little sachet of sweet-smelling perfume in solid form around their necks.

'Henna' (the correct term) is used for dying hair red. En Gedi in the desert, halfway down the western shore of the Dead Sea, was not only well known for its perfumes, but also as an oasis. It was a delightful, private, romantic spot, away from the city. Picture a quiet but bright spot of colour, beauty and life (the flowers in question are white and yellow), of sweet-smelling joy (the aroma is distinct) and of hope in the midst of a desert landscape.

As this woman reclined at the king's table, two things were happening. Firstly, the scent of her perfume was wafting out into the room. His presence was producing a warm and loving response from her. While she was alluring him with her beauty, at the same time he was filling her thoughts. These were like the smell of myrrh, or **'henna blossoms from the vineyards of En Gedi'**.

The idea of **'a sachet of myrrh resting between my breasts'** is evocative (the AV's controversial, 'He shall lie all night betwixt my breasts' even more so). It suggests, on the one hand, intimacy and familiarity and, on the other, continuity or durability. Here it is describing her present devotion to her lover and anticipating something future. One day the king will lie with her, and even now he is close to her heart in that he is always in her thoughts. As they were unmarried at this point they would not have become physically intimate. While having a strong attachment to one another, unmarried couples must take great care to avoid inappropriate intimate physical contact.

On the human plane, this is how prospective wives should think of their prospective husbands. When those strong desires and this hearty devotion are absent, there is something wrong. Commitment is vital.

On the spiritual level, Longman says that Cyril of Alexandria is 'at his creative best' when he sees the two breasts as the Old and New Testaments, with Christ the sachet of myrrh at their heart, and rightly rejects the suggestion! Perhaps we are better to think of Christ welcoming his people to his table, as at the Last Supper. Some may find even this suggestion forced, but remember how John laid his head on Jesus' breast on that occasion. Certainly we all ought to endeavour to draw near to the Saviour and make room for him in our hearts. Paul prays 'that Christ may dwell in your hearts through faith' (Eph. 3:17). For the believer, every thought of Christ should be as of an agreeable perfume, of beautiful fragrance, a bouquet of delight. He has blessed us in every way. How good he has been to us! Do you think of Christ in this way? Is he precious to you? (1 Peter 2:7). Are you submissive to him? Do you want him to come to you? Do you delight in thinking of him, and of all that he has done, and is doing, for you? That is how it should be.

In a letter to the pious Lady Kenmure, on the death of her husband, Samuel Rutherford seeks to use this image and writes, 'Your dearest Lord made you a widow woman for Christ, who is now suiting for marriage love of you. And therefore since you lie alone in your bed, let Christ be as a bundle of myrrh, to sleep and lie all the night betwixt your breasts and then your bed is better filled than before.'

A model of royal fellowship

The final section we want to look at in this chapter is 1:15 –
2:2. It contains an enchanting sequence of brief exchanges,
banter even, between the couple. It is followed in 2:3-13 by
another longer speech from the beloved, which we shall
consider in the next chapter. These verses give us an idea of
the intimacy and love between the betrothed couple as they
compliment one another. The relationship is developing.
There is dialogue, conversation, chit-chat. Here is a fascinating tête-à-tête. As before, there are both horizontal and
vertical lessons.

1. Regards and response

We begin with the lover's expression of his high regard for
her, his compliment:

> **How beautiful you are, my darling!**
> **Oh, how beautiful!**
> **Your eyes are doves**
>
> (1:15).

She responds in kind: '**How handsome you are, my
lover! Oh, how charming!**' (1:16).

The '**darling**' is repeated from 1:9. There are many
references in the book to '**doves**'. The dove, a clean bird in
terms of the law of Moses, symbolizes several things. In this
book it stands particularly for gentleness, purity, chastity and
faithfulness. The exact reference here is unclear. What is in
mind? Is it the whiteness of her eyes, their beauty, their
softness, or their tranquillity? Is it possibly the way that her
eyes dart about, looking in different directions, or that her
eyelashes flutter like doves' wings? We cannot be sure.

The importance of beautiful eyes in a woman is expressed in Genesis 29:17: 'Leah had weak eyes, but Rachel was lovely in form, and beautiful.' Probably drawing on the narratives of the life of Jacob, rabbinic teaching connected beautiful eyes with a beautiful personality. Undoubtedly, this woman is beautiful, but all else we learn of her suggests that she is also gentle, pure and faithful. Her lover is moved by this (note his **'Oh!'** The verse literally begins: 'Look!'). He declares her to be his 'darling', his 'love'.

She in turn is impressed with his good looks and his charm. For the word translated **'charming'** the RSV has 'truly lovely', an effort to bring out the intensity of the Hebrew. The word occurs only ten times in the Old Testament. The first half of 1:15 is identical to the first half of 1:16 in Hebrew except for the fact that 1:16, as the NIV reflects, is in the masculine form. The word is used fourteen times in the book, but this is the only time it is in this masculine form. The woman too is moved (note her echoing **'Oh!'**) and owns him to be her lover.

This is how it should be, to a growing and developing extent, between an engaged couple, and indeed between a man and his wife. There should be mutual praise — adoration and answer, regard and response. It should be sincerely spoken. It is not enough simply to feel it deep down inside and say nothing.

On a higher plane, the relationship between the believer and his Lord ought to be something like this as well. God's Word declares that, however unworthy we may feel, however undeserving, if we are true believers, then Christ is enthralled with us. When he looks into our eyes, as it were, he sees the Holy Spirit and all his work in us and he is enraptured. In response, we ought to confess how wonderful the Lord Jesus is. There is no one more appealing, no one more admirable than he. Have you seen that? If you have not, ask God to show it to you. Ask the Lord to loosen your tongue so that you may be able to speak of such things without awkwardness or embarrassment.

2. Fellowship and freedom

She adds, **'And our bed is verdant.'** They are walking in the fields, as it were, and she is describing the open-air nature of their love. They lie down in the fields with the grass, symbolic of freshness and life, beneath them. He responds in kind in 1:17: **'The beams of our house are cedars; our rafters are firs.'**

Solomon built a palace of cedar for himself and for Pharaoh's daughter, his bride (1 Kings 7). Here, in their minds at least, they are in the woods. The trees around them and above them form a sort of house, or houses (the word is actually plural), for them. This speaks of the fellowship and freedom that they enjoy. They are together and they are free to roam. The trees give off a pleasant scent. The cedar, especially, probably speaks too of permanence. We cannot be totally sure which species is meant. The whole forest is theirs. The repeated **'our'** is also significant. The idea of sharing is important.

Few things epitomize young love better than the picture of a couple walking through the countryside together, sharing the joys of God's creation. Think of a modern example such as the evocative song 'Fields of gold'. It describes lovers walking through fields of barley. 'In his arms she fell as her hair came down among the fields of gold.' The man asks, 'Will you stay with me, will you be my love among the fields of barley?' Such imagery reinforces both the closeness and freedom of a relationship. Love is not, of course, confined to a rural environment and flourishes even in the city.. Poetically and figuratively, however, the countryside brings out the freedom and joy of young love. It is a most good and desirable thing.

It is significant that the world began in a garden and will end with a city that sounds more rural than urban, more of a garden than anything else. Remember how at the beginning, it would seem, Adam and Eve walked with God in the Garden of Eden in the cool of the day. What fellowship there was, what freedom! They were naked but not ashamed, for they had nothing to be ashamed of. It was all lost, of course, with that first sin. However, it can be restored in Jesus Christ. All who put their trust in him can know that fellowship with God restored and that freedom regained in him in a way that will last for ever in paradise. Jesus reminds us that 'The meek will inherit the earth,' and the believer ought to have a sense upon him of his freedom in Christ. 'By his death', Christ has set 'free those who all their lives were held in slavery by their fear of death' (Heb. 2:14,15). When the Son makes us free, we are free indeed. Because we walk with him, all things are ours — not yet in fact, but at least in principle. It all belongs to our Father, and one day we shall inherit it. He wants to share it with us and wants us to enjoy it for ever. It is for freedom that Christ has set us free.

3. Realization and raptures

This leads to the woman's description of herself in 2:1: **'I am a rose of Sharon, a lily of the valleys.'** We often associate this phrase with the Lord Jesus and some commentators take it to be spoken by the lover. Like many others, the NIV takes the view that the beloved is speaking. Both views make sense. The Lord Jesus is certainly most beautiful and often spoke of himself using the words 'I am...'

The **'rose of Sharon'** is not a rose, but a beautiful flower from the fertile coastal Plain of Sharon, or *the* Sharon (the word means 'plain'). This is a low plain on the shoreline south of the sandy hills leading up to Mount Carmel. Once swampland, the whole area came to be marked by its

fecundity and luscious greenery. Some associate the flower
with the sweet-smelling narcissus, others with the crimson
anemone. Iris, crocus, daffodil and other flowers have all
been suggested. We should note, however, that it is a
flower, emphasizing a general description. The **'lily of the
valleys'** is probably not the flower we know by that name,
but an anemone or a lotus. Amaryllis, woodbine and honey-
suckle have also been suggested as the bloom intended.
Again, a common flower is in mind. Perhaps a slightly
tongue-in-cheek paraphrasing is apt: 'Why did you pick
me?' Her words are like those of Jacob ('I am unworthy...',
Gen. 32:10), David ('Who am I, O Sovereign LORD...?',
2 Sam. 7:18) and Elizabeth ('But why am I so favoured...?', Luke 1:43) as they too ponder the wonder of
God's undeserved goodness. What is our response?

The woman is still modest, but her self-image has im-
proved, in the light of her lover's words. That is a lesson in
itself. What a difference we can make to others merely by
how we speak to them and about them! We ought to give
thought to this. There is no need to lie or to butter people up.
We just need to be quicker than we tend to be to give praise
where praise is due. One reason why we grow discouraged in
the Christian life is our failure to notice how highly the Bible
speaks of believers. What wonderful things it says! (see Ps.
87:3). Do you not realize, believer, that you are a flower in
God's garden, a blossom that he himself has planted, placed
there to show forth his glory and beauty? Every time you
praise him that is what you are doing — declaring his splendour. Not even Solomon in all his glory compares.

Can you sing with Samuel Crossman the song of love
unknown, the Saviour's love to you, 'Love to the loveless
shown, that they might lovely be'? Sing:

O who am I,
That for my sake

My Lord should take
Frail flesh and die?

Sing too, with a later writer, Daniel Whittle:

I know not why God's wondrous grace
To me he hath made known,
Nor why, unworthy, Christ in love
Redeemed me for his own.

Finally, notice the king's response: **'Like a lily among thorns is my darling among the maidens'** (2:2). He not only agrees with his beloved, but he playfully adds to her description. 'Yes, you are a lily,' he says, 'like a lily among thorns.' Compared with the other maidens, Solomon has eyes only for this one. She stands out. The others are thorns in comparison, nothing but briers and thistles.

That is how it should be between a prospective husband and wife or a married couple. For the man, his intended, or his wife, should be not only a lily, but also an outstanding lily. The charms of others must hold no real allure for him. For him they are to be mere thorns in comparison. She must always have the highest place in his affections and in his thinking.

That is certainly how it is between Jesus and his people. In his eyes, we are lilies amid thorns. There is no question that there is a sense in which he loves everyone (see, for example, Ps. 145:9; Matt. 5:45) yet there is a special love that Christ has for his own, his lilies among the thorns. He says of the ungodly, 'The best of them is like a brier, the most upright worse than a thorn hedge' (Micah 7:4), but those he saves are lilies. They 'shine like stars in the universe' (Phil. 2:15).

Do you realize that this is how the Lord sees you, believer? You stand out for him as special. You are his chosen one and though you may not always feel like it, you ought to. Indeed, we must remember to stand out for him as lilies among thorns. 'I am a rose of Sharon,' you can say, 'a lily of the valley. I have been chosen in him before the foundation of the world. He has passed others by, but not me. He has given me the Spirit of Christ and he is working all things together for my good. Even now I am a child of God and what I will be has not yet been made known, but it will be something wonderfully glorious.' This is not a prescription for a course in positive thinking, but a description of biblical faith — taking God at his word and believing the promises that he makes. That is what we must do. What an impact it would make!

In Spurgeon's day there were people who sought to brighten up the lives of the poor by bringing them flowers. Spurgeon does not oppose such flower missions but, he says, 'They do better still who are themselves flowers in the places where they live.'

The thorns all around us want to choke the good seed and are a source of distress to us — messengers of Satan that whip our backs and are a pain in our eyes and sides — but we should not be afraid. Remember God's words to his prophet Ezekiel: 'Do not be afraid, though briers and thorns are all around you and you live among scorpions. Do not be afraid of what they say or terrified by them...' (Ezek. 2:6). Soon these thorns will be burnt up. Evil people will be 'cast aside like thorns, which are not gathered with the hand ... burned up where they lie' (2 Sam. 23:6,7).

And if you are not a believer, ask him to make you a rose of Sharon. Ask him to make you a lily of the valley. By nature we are all thorns — unproductive and useless, un-scented and dull, hard and twisted, sharp and ugly. But he can change us. He can make us attractive, fragrant, kind, luxuriant, straight, tender, useful and vibrant, through what was done on the cross. At that time Christ wore the crown of thorns and suffered and died so that all who believe in him may be beautiful in his sight and live a life of love for his glory. Perhaps it is a little fanciful, but Spurgeon speaks of the lacerations Christ suffered in gathering his lilies. With George Matheson we sing:

> O love that will not let me go,
> I rest my weary soul in thee!

We lay down our life's glory dead in the dust:

> And from the ground there blossoms red
> Life that shall endless be.

To sum up

It is important for men to assure their beloved ones of their love through appropriate words and deeds. Beloved ones should appreciate such reassurance. Strong desire and devotion ought to characterize a woman's attitude to her man. Mutual commitment and devotion are vital. Reciprocal praise should feature too. How we speak to and about each other can have a significant impact. Once in a relationship, all other charms must be resisted. Your wife, or wife-to-be, must always come first in your thinking.

Christ is enthralled with his people. He gives them good gifts and he works to present them to himself without fault. We, for our part, must seek always to draw near to him. Every thought of Christ, who has blessed us in every way, should be a joy. How good he is! How great his love for us! All things are his and one day we shall inherit. We are to enjoy him always. We become discouraged when we forget how positively the Bible speaks of believers. Jesus has a special love for his own. Always remember that vital fact.

5.
Coming together: The nature of true love

Please read Song of Songs 2:3-17

'After you've watched *Human Senses* your world will never feel the same again.' So claimed a BBC press release promoting a series presented by zoologist Nigel Marven. 'On a sensory romp around the globe,' it adds, 'Nigel acts as a human guinea pig, experiencing first-hand the extremes of sensory perception — from sound so wonderful it makes him grin with pleasure to a smell so awful it brings him out in a sweat and sets his heart racing.' They also promise footage of Nigel swimming with sharks, tackling an alligator and coming face to face with an angry cobra!

Apart from their evolutionary assumptions, my eldest son and I enjoyed the programmes we saw, with their state-of-the-art graphics and occasional 'invasive imaging techniques'. God has given most of us what we traditionally refer to as the five senses — sight, sound, smell, touch and taste. An educationalist's dream, the senses are often dealt with.

When reading the Bible we tend to use only one or two senses. Perhaps the first thing to note about chapter 2 of the Song of Songs, however, is the striking way in which it is filled with sensual imagery — even more so than chapter 1. To get to grips with it, we need somehow not only to *see* what is described — trees, fruit, gazelles, hills, banqueting halls, and so on — but also, as it were, to hear, smell, taste and feel it — the noise of a banqueting hall, or the cooing of doves; the fragrance of the lilies, or the scent of the night air; the delicious taste of grapes, or of refreshing apples.

There is an *inclusio*, or bracketing, in 2:8-17 — the passage is enclosed within two identical, or very similar, phrases: 'like a gazelle or a young stag'. The whole section, 2:3-17, teaches several things about true love. The pattern of the conversation is probably as follows:

Shulammite	Friends	Solomon
2:3-10a	—	—
2:10b-13 (quoting the lover's words)	—	2:10b-13 (in quotation)
	—	2:14-15
2:16-17	—	—

True love — desire and patience

1. True love holds its object in high esteem

In 2:3-13 the beloved speaks again. She begins, **'Like an apple tree among the trees of the forest is my lover among the young men.'** This motif recurs in 8:5. This is the image that the woman uses to describe her lover. There is an interesting parallel with what he has said of her, when he described her as a lily among thorns. In true love, lovers must see one another as unique. It does not matter how tall or grand or ancient, how beautiful or striking, other trees may be — she has eyes only for her apple tree.

This **'apple tree'**, or probably some other fruit tree (oranges, apricots or pomegranates have been suggested), does two things there in the potentially inhospitable forest. It provides restful shade and it bears delicious fruit. Therefore, it stands out among the trees of the forest. She says, **'I delight to sit in his shade, and his fruit is sweet to my taste'** (2:3). To be in the presence of her lover gives pure contentment — it is both pleasant and edifying. He offers protection and pleasure, defence and delight.

Down to more recent times apple trees have graced many a love song, as in 'Don't sit under the apple tree with anyone else but me,' or the quirky 'Bony Maronie', which talks of 'making love under the apple tree'. As one writer points out, the reference here is erotic but not explicit.

Do you hold your love in high esteem? Is your fiancé or spouse someone you regard highly and respect? Are you happy to be in his shade, so to speak? Further, is there a longing for intimacy with him (or with her)? Are you eager for the fruit he (or she) can offer? That is how it should be between prospective husband and wife, or man and wife.

On another level, do you hold Christ in high esteem? Do you see that he is unique? Do you think of him as an apple tree compared with other trees? Do you long for intimacy with him? Do you long to know his shelter and comfort, enjoying the fruit of the Spirit that he alone can give? He is 'your shade at your right hand' if you are his (Ps. 121:5). 'Taste and see that the LORD is good' (Ps. 34:8). Can you echo the following words by the Scots preacher Ralph Erskine?

> What fool soever disagrees,
> My sweet experience proves
> That Jesus is the tree of trees
> Among a thousand groves.

John Owen wrote, 'When the heat of wrath is ready to scorch the soul, Christ, interposing, bears it all. Under the shadow of his wings we sit down ... putting our trust in him ... with great delight.'

This verse inspired Frances Ridley Havergal's hymn which begins:

> Sit down beneath his shadow,
> And rest with great delight;
> The faith that now beholds him
> Is pledge of future sight.
>
> Bring every weary burden,
> Thy sin, thy fear, thy grief;
> He calls the heavy laden,
> And gives them kind relief.

He can protect you from harm and feed you like no other. Go to him always.

2. True love looks forward to intimacy

In 2:4-6 the beloved expresses her longings for intimacy as she looks forward to that coming point in her relationship with her lover. She is full of anticipation and expectation as she looks forward to such familiarity. How eagerly she longs for what is ahead! She waits with confidence, with aching and with longing.

Confidence

'He has taken me to the banquet hall, and his banner over me is love' (2:4). Many Christians have enjoyed singing this verse in recent years, but what does it mean? At Jewish weddings the bride and groom marry under a canopy (*chuppah*). This could be what is referred to, but it is a **'banner'** that is specifically mentioned. Today banners are relatively rare. In days gone by they were more common, especially when soldiers went into hand-to-hand battle. A regiment's colours, an army's standard, its insignia, served as a rallying point for the troops, being easy to see at a distance. One sometimes sees them hanging in British cathedrals and churches. In Numbers 2:2 we read how Israel was to 'camp round the Tent of Meeting some distance from it, each man under his standard with the banners of his family'. This seems to be the allusion. Possibly the idea of authority and possession, as in the act of planting the flag to claim land, lurks here too.

She envisages the king taking her into his **'banquet hall'**, or more literally, his 'house of wine', a phrase that occurs only here. Is it referring to vines, or does it imply a change of scene, a move indoors? Wine speaks of joy and gladness. It has already been established as indicative of love. The king leads her in as a person of great importance. He heads a procession with a streamer declaring their love. The message is not so much 'Make love not war' as 'Make love your war' or 'Strive for love'. This is a public thing, then, something very open. The woman is confident about the fact that that is how it is and how it will be. A love affair should almost always be like that. It does not have to be accompanied by fanfares and the full glare of publicity, but it should be something that is known, that is in the public domain. It should not be conducted in a clandestine or covert manner. More often than not, if it is kept secret this is because there is something illicit about it, or there is a problem on one side or the other. Obviously, something may begin secretly and there is need for discretion and decorum, but it should not normally continue to remain a secret for any length of time.

This applies both to human love and to love for Jesus Christ. If you love someone you should be confident that the other person will own up to it too. If there are good grounds for the fear that he or she would deny it when asked to acknowledge it, that relationship is going nowhere. It needs either to be put on a better footing or else to be abandoned.

Similarly, there ought to be openness about our love to Christ. There are examples of secret disciples in Scripture — Nicodemus and Joseph of Arimathea seem to have been in that category for a while, but circumstances compelled them to come into the open and they willingly acknowledged the Lord. Anyone who truly loves the Lord will want to be open and honest about it. Christ certainly shows no shame in owning the names of those who follow him and honouring them. Though they are nothing but poor country girls, as it were, he welcomes them into his banqueting house. His love for them is evident to all.

James Durham says, 'It is only the love of Christ that secures believers in their battles and march against their spiritual adversaries.'

The image of the **'banquet hall'** is itself very rich, especially when we think of Christ. To become a Christian is to enter Christ's banqueting house and to be under his banner of love. It is to feast in his palace of pleasure, confident of his undying devotion. What rich delights, what ecstasies there!

In 1836 American Roswell Park's communion hymn reflected in this way:

> Jesus spreads his banner o'er us,
> Cheers our famished souls with food;
> He the banquet spreads before us,
> Of his mystic flesh and blood.
> Precious banquet, bread of heaven,
> Wine of gladness, flowing free;
> May we taste it, kindly given,
> In remembrance, Lord, of thee.

Aching

She goes on:

Strengthen me with raisins,
   refresh me with apples,
   for I am faint with love

(2:5).

The latter phrase is also used in 5:8. When people fall in
love, it is common enough for them to be unable to eat or to
grow faint with love, to be lovesick, as we would say. The
emotional turmoil has a physical effect on them. The beloved
cannot take much more of this and asks for food of some
kind to sustain her (or possibly for flowers to revive her with
their scent, or for something on which to rest). The refreshing apples are obviously from her lover.

Many know about lovesickness on the human level, but
what about achings for Christ? Have you ever been almost ill
in your desperation to meet with Christ? Why are our longings and achings for him not greater? Think of some of the
things that David says in the psalms:

As the deer pants for streams of water,
   so my soul pants for you, O God.
My soul thirsts for God, for the living God.
   When can I go and meet with God?

(Ps. 42:1-2).

O God, you are my God,
   earnestly I seek you;
my soul thirsts for you,
   my body longs for you,

in a dry and weary land
    where there is no water

(Ps. 63:1).

How lovely is your dwelling-place,
    O LORD Almighty!
My soul yearns, even faints,
    for the courts of the LORD;
my heart and my flesh cry out
    for the living God

(Ps. 84:1-2).

That is how we should ache for God.

Longing

In 2:6 the woman describes lying down with her lover so that **'His left arm is under my head, and his right arm embraces me.'** The verse, repeated in 8:3, contains no verbs in Hebrew, and so the tense is ambiguous. It could describe sexual intercourse, but may represent an intimate embrace. If the former, she is longing for this moment rather than describing what is happening, or has happened, as this is before they marry. She certainly craves intimacy with her lover. She longs for his nearness and his support in her weakness, which he gives. Like Peter sinking in the waves, she needs upholding.

On the human level, it is right that confident assurance be accompanied by longings for intimacy. There is something wrong if such feelings are absent. They need to be handled carefully, undoubtedly, but should be present.

On the spiritual level, it is also right that confident assurance be matched by longings for intimacy. Do we long to draw nearer to Christ? Do we cry with William Cowper, 'O for a closer walk with God!' or pray with Fanny Crosby:

'Draw me nearer, nearer, nearer, blessed Lord,
To the place where thou hast died.
Draw me nearer, nearer, nearer, blessed Lord,
To thy precious, bleeding side'?

We ought to.

3. True love always shows great patience

But then comes the balance. The beloved turns to the daughters of Jerusalem and sounds a warning note:

Daughters of Jerusalem, I charge you
  by the gazelles and by the does of the field:
Do not arouse or awaken love
  until it so desires

(2:7).

This refrain recurs in 3:5 and 8:4 (see also 5:8).

It is not clear exactly what she means by the oath. It has been pointed out that the Hebrew words translated as **'by the gazelles and by the does of the field'** sound a little like names for God and may contain a veiled reference to him. The reference to female deer matches others elsewhere to male deer and is perhaps an appropriate image for fertility, devotion and patience. The request not to **'arouse or awaken'** is not a 'Do not disturb' label for the lovers. Rather, it is a reminder that, when talking about such feelings, we must always be careful. We all have them to some extent, these desires and needs. The world says, 'If it feels good, do it.' It urges us to go with our feelings, often regardless of all else. That is a recipe for disaster. There are great problems with attempting to go down that road. We are sinners and it is the easiest thing in the world for such feelings to become impure and improper and to lead us astray.

Further, there is the whole matter of timing. In any relationship obviously two people are involved and so there is a need for co-ordination. Even the simplest things, like walking down a road arm in arm, or sharing an umbrella, are, for some, not as easy as they may appear. Certainly the whole process of becoming one — living under the same roof, sharing the same bed — is a major undertaking. You cannot assume that just any person who happens to take your fancy can become your husband or wife as easily as that. People who entertain that belief are bound to run into heartache. Difficulty and disaster, sorrow and sadness loom. No, it is important to take care not to 'arouse or awaken love until it so desires'. Love is a tender plant. It needs to develop at its own pace. When people try to rush things it is a little like the boy who decided to help the butterfly out of the chrysalis — it does not work.

Even the world has some idea of this. Lamont Dozier and Edward and Brian Holland formed a successful popular music-writing team in the sixties. In one song a young woman bewails her loneliness and longing for love in these terms:

> How long must I wait,
> how much more must I take,
> before loneliness
> will cause my heart to break?

She feels she cannot bear living alone any longer and is impatient for true love. This leads her to say that, when she feels she can't go on, certain precious words keep her hanging on. And so the chorus goes:

I remember mama said, 'You can't hurry love.
No, you'll just have to wait.'
She said, 'Love don't come easy.
It's a game of give and take.'

Perhaps that final sentiment needs rephrasing, but otherwise she sounds a wise mother.

We must not forget to let children be children. They are under great pressure today to grow up too quickly. Younger people should not be unduly anxious about whom they will marry, or similar questions. God willing, there will be plenty of time to think about such things later. There is evidence to say that much of the sex education in state schools in Britain today only encourages promiscuity and increases the likelihood of teenage pregnancy. 'Unfortunately,' as a forthright newspaper columnist lamented in 2004, 'it's seen as politically incorrect to say that teenage promiscuity is disastrous...'

Mostly in America, but also in Britain, there have been campaigns, some of them with government backing, encouraging pledges of abstinence from sex until marriage. 'True love waits,' and the 'Silver ring thing' are the best known. They have seen limited success. Such pledges can make a crucial difference, but it is the Spirit's work alone that facilitates lasting purity.

Are you an unmarried person who would like to be married? Be patient. Wait! 'Do not arouse or awaken love until it so desires.' Some people never marry. Bear that possibility in mind. If the thought appals you, keep in mind that God's grace is sufficient.

Are you a married person? Married people need to be patient too — in a different way, of course, but impatience, not waiting until the right moment, will lead to frustration and pain too. Where a marriage is in decay, patience is especially needed so that it can be recovered, or if beyond repair dissolved in God's good time. Where it is thriving, patience is still necessary in order for it to be even more fruitful.

Are you a believer? We all need to be patient, living, as we do, in this 'now-and-not-yet' period. Like young unmarried lovers, we have already met with Christ. We know him and walk with him. However, we await the wedding day. We are looking forward to his return — the consummation of all things. Until then, patience is vital. We must be calm and quiet, submissive and serene, whatever provocations come, as we long for Christ's return.

True love — wanting to be together

In 2:8-13 the beloved continues to speak. She describes the coming of her lover and how he speaks to her. Again the passage is full of instruction on both the horizontal and vertical planes.

1. How a true lover comes to his beloved

> **Listen! My lover!**
>   **Look! Here he comes,**
> **leaping across the mountains,**
>   **bounding over the hills.**
> **My lover is like a gazelle or a young stag.**
>   **Look! There he stands behind our wall,**
> **gazing through the windows,**
>   **peering through the lattice**
>
> (2:8-9).

Urging us to use our eyes and ears, the woman imagines him coming to visit her. It works on three levels. Metaphorically, he is a leaping gazelle. More literally, he bounds across the hills, probably on horseback, and then knocks at her door, eager to be admitted. Beyond that is an even more intimate picture of him coming very close to her physically. The keynotes are energy, enthusiasm, eagerness and excitement.

Is that how you come to your beloved? From first to last in a relationship such fervour and passion should be present. Obviously it is more noticeable early on, but it should never be entirely lost. This is how the Lord Jesus comes to his people. Nothing was allowed to prevent his incarnation and by his Spirit he continues to visit his people today. Too often we come sluggishly and slowly, at the pace of a snail or a tortoise. Motivation is often lacking. But not so with Christ:

> O'er hills of guilt and seas of grief,
> He leaps, he flies to my relief.

He bounds like a gazelle over the hills that stand between us, hills of indifference and sin. They seem to us to bar the way, but he springs over every barrier in a leap and comes to us.

He stands at the door and knocks, longing to be admitted. He peers into our very souls, so eager is he for intimacy. What a lover he is! Yet how slow we are to appreciate him and desire him! Our views of him are often obscured and distorted, but these verses assure us that he is most eager to meet with us.

2. How a true lover speaks to his beloved

In 2:10-13 the beloved quotes her lover, or imagines what he would say. An apparent *inclusio* appears here — the passage opens with, **'Arise, my darling, my beautiful one, and come with me'** (2:10), and concludes with, **'Arise, come, my darling; my beautiful one, come with me'** (2:13). What beautiful poetry he pours forth from beyond the confining wall! He has come to her and now, as he stands there in the open country, he wants her to come to him.

She says:

My lover spoke and said to me,
  'Arise, my darling,
  my beautiful one, and come with me...'

(**'With me'** is not in the Hebrew but is in the Septuagint). This is the burden of his message. He speaks to his **'beautiful one'**. She has been indoors too long. The winter weather has kept her inside. He takes hold of her, lifts her up and takes her outside with him.

See! [he says] **The winter is past;**
  the rains are over and gone.
Flowers appear on the earth;
  the season of singing [the word can also mean
    'pruning'] **has come,**
the cooing of doves
  is heard in our land.
The fig-tree forms its early fruit;
  the blossoming vines spread their fragrance.
Arise, come, my darling;
  my beautiful one, come with me.

It is springtime! Spring has sprung. The winter rains are gone. Look at the flowers! Listen to the doves cooing! Smell the flowers and the fruit on the trees! Taste the vernal air, the freshness in the atmosphere! Feel the warmth of the sunshine! In the minds of poets spring has long been associated with falling in love. In 'Locksley Hall' Tennyson famously wrote of how 'In the Spring a young man's fancy lightly turns to thoughts of love.' Love is sometimes called 'spring fever', as spring is often the time of year when young men wake up to realize that there are beautiful young women about. All through the winter they have hardly noticed them,

but now, in the sunshine, the girls seem to be maturing and
blossoming. The connection between spring and love is no
doubt the idea of freshness and beauty, liveliness and colour.
When two people are in love, whether it is winter or summer,
spring is in the air — everything is alive and bright, animated
and intense.

Matthew Henry makes a fivefold spiritual application
here. Spring is like the coming in of the gospel age in which
we now are. What an era in which to be living! Isaac Watts
wrote that:

> The Jewish wintry state is gone,
> The mists are fled, the spring comes on;
> The sacred turtle-dove we hear
> Proclaim the new, the joyful year.
>
> Th' immortal vine of heav'nly root
> Blossoms, and buds, and gives her fruit:
> Lo! We are come to taste the wine;
> Our souls rejoice, and bless the vine.

Matthew Henry also says that whenever the church is
delivered from a period of persecution, it is like springtime.
We are to give thanks for such deliverances.

Conversion itself is a passage from the cold, hard, frozen
winter of unbelief to the warmer, thawed climes of a spring
where buds shoot and sprout everywhere. Even after conversion there can be relatively wintry periods but, in God's
goodness, seasons of refreshing come and it is spring again.
Finally, there will be 'an eternal farewell to winter and a
joyful entrance upon an everlasting spring' at the resurrection.

Have you heard the voice of Jesus speaking in his Word
lately? 'Arise, my darling,' he says, 'my beautiful one, and
come with me.' He can banish the dolefulness and drudgery
of winter. He brings hope and joy, vitality and vigour into

your life, if you simply let him take your hand. He does that for the unbeliever who comes to trust in him for the first time. He does it again and again when he renews and refreshes those who are in him. He makes everything new. Oh, look to him and be transformed!

Remember his words in Luke 21:28-31: 'When these things begin to take place, stand up and lift up your heads, because your redemption is drawing near. He told them this parable: "Look at the fig-tree and all the trees. When they sprout leaves, you can see for yourselves and know that summer is near. Even so, when you see these things happening, you know that the kingdom of God is near."'

The eighteenth-century Baptist pastor Benjamin Beddome wrote:

> Great God, thou author of the spring,
> Thy love our songs demands...

He pleaded:

> Enliven, Lord, our languid souls,
> There shed thy beams again;
> Nor let us like the frozen poles
> In barrenness remain.

In 1889 Jackson Mason's 'O voice of the Beloved!' appeared. The lover calls to his beloved to 'Arise and come away. For lo, 'tis past ... the winter of thy year.' Having set the scene, he writes:

> Yea, Lord! Thy passion over,
> We know this life of ours
> Hath passed from death and winter
> To leaves and budding flowers;
> No more thy rain of weeping

In drear Gethsemane;
No more the clouds and darkness,
That veiled thy bitter tree.
Our Easter Sun is risen!
And yet we slumber long,
And need thy Dove's sweet pleading
To waken prayer and song.
Oh, breathe upon our deadness,
Oh, shine upon our gloom;
Lord, let us feel thy presence
And rise and live and bloom.

True love — four tests

In 2:14-17, it seems, the lover speaks first, then the beloved. Their words draw out four basic characteristics, or tests, of true love.

1. The desire test

If it is true love, you want to see and hear your beloved.

The lover begins by saying, **'My dove in the clefts of the rock, in the hiding-places on the mountainside,'** then, appealing again to sight and sound, he uses a chiasmus, or X-shaped arrangement:

> **Show me your *face*,**
>   **let me hear your *voice*;**
> **for your *voice* is sweet,**
>   **and your *face* is lovely**

                                                                   (2:14).

The image is of a rock pigeon hiding in the clefts of a rocky hill. The lover imagines his beloved is such a creature.

This loving and peaceable woman is inaccessible and in a barren place at present but he wants to find her. He wants to see and hear her. Nearness and fruitfulness will follow. Her inaccessibility fans the flame of his ardour. He loves the sound of her voice, so sweet to his ear. He loves the look of her form or face, so lovely to see. The Hebrew word is actually plural, 'faces' — he loves her every expression, all aspects of her character.

Now this may seem a little obvious, but in true love the lovers like to look at each other and hear each other's voice. Sometimes an irrational fear will come over a single Christian: 'What if the Lord wants me to marry someone I don't like the look of, or whose voice I can't stand?' But no, when the Lord calls two people to marry he expects them to like the way they look and sound to each other. These are not the only factors, of course, but they are important. If you are going to spend forty or fifty years with a person, it is best that you find him or her pleasant to look at and sweet to listen to.

God has so made us that we all have different faces and voices. Some are more obviously beautiful than others, but beauty is in the eye of the beholder, as they say. Of course, the beauty of a voice or face can be lost. There is a warning in Proverbs: 'Better to live on a corner of the roof than share a house with a quarrelsome wife' (Prov. 21:9; 25:24).

On a more spiritual level, remember that the Lord loves to see us and hear us, no matter how ugly we look or how croaky we sound. Here is an encouragement to come to him and worship him, and especially to pray to him.

Thy voice to me sounds ever sweet;
My graces in thy count'nance meet;
Though the vain world thy face despise,
'Tis bright and comely in mine eyes.

It is hard to imagine how the Lord can have any delight in hearing us, but we know, especially those who are parents, how delightful it is to see and hear a small child ask questions and talk to us. Perhaps we should think of it in similar terms. More appropriately in this context, there is the way 'sweet nothings' can be spoken in a lover's ear and give great joy. I remember how in my courting days I ran up huge telephone bills on the line from London to Aberystwyth. What did we find to talk about for so long? Nothing, really. Just to talk was enough. If only we had the same desires to pray and worship as we can have for one another. We ought to respond with Watts:

> Dear Lord, our thankful heart receives
> The hope thine invitation gives;
> To thee our joyful lips shall raise
> The voice of prayer and of praise.

2. The determination test

If it is true love, you will determine to deal with anything that might mar the relationship.

Now comes a warning note:

> **Catch for us the foxes,**
> **the little foxes**
> **that ruin the vineyards,**
> **our vineyards that are in bloom**

                                                        (2:15).

Garrett calls the verse 'a major enigma'. There are various views. Is it the woman saying she has lost her virginity? Is it a call to tame the wildness of sexual experience? Is it a reference to lustful boys taking advantage of innocent girls?

Or is it a call to deal with anything that may hinder her feminine charm, or their mutual love from blooming?

I take the last of these views. The vineyards stand for the lovers. It is spring and the vines are in bloom. It is a happy time. But what if the foxes, especially the little ones, sneak in and start eating the grapes? They must be dealt with. The lover does not say, 'I'll catch them.' Rather he instructs his beloved that she should **'catch for us the foxes'**. In other words, 'You deal with them, for both our sakes.' Or perhaps it should be: 'Let us catch...' These foxes symbolize the various, sometimes relatively little, things that can creep in and play havoc with a fruitful relationship. Think of the little foxes of jealousy, lack of self-control, selfishness, mistrust, pride and unwillingness to forgive. Such little foxes need to be caught before they do damage. A cuddly little cub can soon grow into a vicious, dangerous wild animal. A small problem in marriage can grow until it threatens to drive a couple apart.

London has a large urban fox population. We see them in the garden from time to time and have even been kept awake at night by their noise. I was walking through the park at the end of our street one night when suddenly I was confronted by a little fox. It is an unnerving experience. One assumes it will run away like a cat, but then the thought comes: 'What if it comes at me?' As for catching a fox, that cannot be easy. They have sharp teeth!

We need to be careful. Such predators need to be dealt with, however. It is no good saying, 'Oh it is only a little one!' Little foxes grow into big ones. Even little foxes can do damage. Hunt them down. Remove the threat. Kill them before they ruin you. As John Owen put it in his wonderful treatise on mortification of sin, 'Be killing sin or it will be killing you.'

3. The duality test

If it is true love, there will be mutual feelings of love.

Here is another famous verse: **'My lover is mine and I am his; he browses among the lilies'** (2:16). It is very simple. There is mutual love here. He loves me; I love him. I belong to him; he belongs to me.

> In a love which cannot cease,
> I am his and he is mine.

Many today do not like to think of marriage in terms of one partner owning the other. Yet what could be more romantic than a covenant of love between two people in which he is hers and she is his?

Perhaps it is best to picture him here as a stag or a gazelle again, but now, instead of bounding towards her, he is grazing among the lilies. Where there is real love its pace varies — there are times of great passion and times of calm, quiet reflection. In the light of 5:13, perhaps we can think of these lilies as her lips, or maybe the lilies speak of his people. Perhaps we should simply think of him as a strong and manly one who is yet surrounded by beauty.

Spurgeon often preached on this verse. On one occasion he spoke of a delighting to have Christ ('My lover is mine'), a delighting to belong to Christ ('… and I am his') and a delight in the very thought of Christ ('He browses among the lilies'). At another time the text prompted pertinent questions such as: 'Have you taken hold of Christ by faith? Is he truly your Lover, the Lover of your soul? Is he dear to you above all your possessions? Do you love him more than any earthly friend? Do you have no other hope or trust but him? Do your thoughts go after him? Will you own up to all this?'

Do you have a confident love towards Christ? It is a great prize, one we ought to covet. In 1872 Charles E. Mudie's *Stray leaves* included this hymn:

I lift my heart to thee, Saviour divine;
For thou art all to me, and I am thine;
Is there on earth a closer bond than this,
That my Beloved's mine, and I am his?

Thine am I by all ties; but chiefly thine,
That through thy sacrifice thou, Lord, art mine.
By thine own cords of love, so sweetly wound,
Around me, I to thee am closely bound.

To thee, thou bleeding Lamb, I all things owe —
All that I have, and am, and all I know.
All that I have is now no longer mine,
And I am not mine own; Lord, I am thine.

How can I, Lord, withhold life's brightest hour
From thee; or gathered gold, or any power?
Why should I keep one precious thing from thee;
When thou hast giv'n thine own dear self for me?

I pray thee, Saviour, keep me in thy love,
Until death's holy sleep shall me remove
To that fair realm where, sin and sorrow o'er,
Thou and thine own are one for evermore.

4. The development test

If it is true love, you will long for even greater intimacy.

Finally, switching from the third to the second person (*enallage* again, as in 1:2-4), she once more anticipates the day of consummation:

Until the day breaks [breathes]
  and the shadows flee,
turn, my lover,
  and be like a gazelle
or like a young stag
  on the rugged hills

(2:17).

Again she imagines her lover as a gazelle or young stag coming to her. Now he browses among the lilies, but soon he will come for her. He will gambol on the **'rugged** [or possibly 'divided'] **hills'**. She looks forward to it.

This is how husband and wife should think of one another when apart. This is how young lovers, with all chastity, should look forward to their wedding day. This is how Old Testament believers looked forward to Christ's first coming. They waited as 'people walking in darkness' until they saw the 'great light' dawn. As believers we should look forward to Christ's return. Are we looking forward like that? Do we long for that glorious wedding day? 2 Peter 3:12 speaks of believers looking forward to, or waiting eagerly for, 'the day of God to come', or speeding its coming. Christ will come suddenly like a thief. Meanwhile believers eagerly wait for him to be revealed (1 Cor. 1:7). Their blessed hope is 'the glorious appearing of our great God and Saviour, Jesus Christ' (Titus 2:13). They wait 'for the mercy of our Lord Jesus Christ to bring [them] to eternal life' (Jude 21).

O come, thou Dayspring, come and cheer,
Our spirits by thine advent here;
Disperse the gloomy clouds of night,
And death's dark shadows put to flight.

To sum up

If you truly love someone, you will not only long for that person, but also hold him or her in high esteem. Respect is vital in any productive relationship. Unmarried lovers look forward to intimacy with confidence, aching and longing, but also with patience. They let the tender plant, love, grow at its own pace. If unmarried, be patient. If married, wait for the right moment. True love waits. From first to last, relationships need enthusiasm on both sides.

Do you hold Christ in high regard, seeing him as unique? If you love Christ, then be open about it. Christians are in Christ's banqueting house under his banner of love. Do we long to draw nearer to him? In this 'now-and-not-yet' period before his return we need patience, whatever provocations may come. Even now Christ is eager to meet with us. Have you heard him in his Word? He brings life and joy and every blessing. With him victory is certain.

All true love is marked by a desire to see and hear the one you love, by a resolve to deal with anything that may mar the relationship, by mutual feelings of love and by longings for ever greater intimacy. This is true on both the horizontal and vertical planes.

6.
Crisis: A lover lost, a lover sought, a lover found

Please read Song of Songs 3:1-5

As we turn to chapter 3, we become aware of a marked change of mood. The atmosphere is very different. There is also a change of theme. While 3:1 marks a new phase, most commentators also rightly see a significant break between 3:5 and 3:6. What we read in 1:1 – 3:5 really deals with the courtship between the beloved and her lover, the woman and the man. Up to 3:5 it is all anticipation. However, from 3:6 onwards we are dealing with the wedding day itself and beyond.

Chapter 3 divides, then, into two obvious parts, one coming before the wedding, the other after it. In 3:1-5 we find a theme that will recur with greater intensity in chapter 5, that of 'a lover lost and found'. It is a matter that has already been touched on. The sequence — absence, longing, search, discovery, joy — has already been suggested in the opening chapters. Here we shall confine our remarks to the relatively short section 3:1-5. We shall consider the similarly brief section 3:6-11, where for the first time we see the two lovers married, in the next chapter. The NIV is probably right to see the woman as sole speaker throughout chapter 3 of the Song:

Shulammite	Friends	Solomon
3:1-5	—	—

Both in this chapter and the next, while not entirely ignoring more mundane issues, I want particularly to emphasize the vertical aspect — lessons about a relationship with the Lord. Here we discover very useful teaching regarding the experience of spiritual desertion and, in the chapter that follows, about the wedding procession that is the Christian life.

Three consecutive experiences emerge here.

The distressing experience of being a lover lost

Some writers find dreams everywhere in the Song. One psychiatrist even used it as a text to teach Freudian dream interpretation! I believe that there are very few dream sequences in the book, but that there is one here. Not all take this view, but because chapter 3 begins, **'All night long on my bed'**, or perhaps 'Night after night on my bed' (the word for **'night'** is plural) and because of the rather surreal atmosphere discernible in verses 1-5, I am persuaded that these verses describe a dream, or a series of recurring dreams.

Our dream life can be a fascinating subject. Salvador Dali observed that 'While we are asleep in this world, we are awake in another one.' That world has a certain amount of inscrutability about it. It is only in the last forty or fifty years that it has been studied closely, following Kleitman and Aserinsky's observation of rapid eye movement in sleep. For whatever reason, it would seem that when we go into a deep sleep, dreaming takes place. Sometimes we remember these dreams; sometimes not. Often they are half remembered, half forgotten. Sometimes we appear to have forgotten a dream until something happens to trigger the memory and we recall

all or part of what we dreamt. Light sleepers tend to remember dreams best; heavier sleepers rarely do.

For lovers a great question can be: 'Did you dream about your loved one?' The idea is that if you are thinking about your loved one every waking hour, then it is no surprise that you think about him or her when you are asleep too. There are even old wives' tales about how to make sure you dream about your lover by following certain superstitious procedures. On the eve of St Agnes, 20 January, for example, they say you should take a row of pins and pull them out, one after the other; then stick a pin in your sleeve. On St Valentine's Day, 14 February, the old superstition involves pinning bay leaves to the pillow to guarantee dreams of your lover, present or future. Such are the absurd workings of human nature!

In reality, even the most ardent lovers sometimes find that they never dream of their beloved ones, or at least that they cannot remember the dreams. Worse than that — and perhaps this has happened to you — they do dream about their loved one, but the dream is disturbing and unsatisfying. This seems to be the case here, initially. Such a phenomenon is especially common where, as in this passage, the wedding day is fast approaching and there are understandable nerves and fears. At such times people often have what psychologists call fear-fulfilment dreams — not exactly nightmares, but something close to them. Nothing seems to go right. The prospective bride dreams she turns up in a tatty old dress; the groom imagines arriving only to be told that his bride has not turned up, and so on. In the nineteenth century Charlotte Brontë used the idea as a literary device in her novel *Jane Eyre*. Before her ill-fated wedding ceremony the heroine dreams ominously of a storm, a wailing child, a missing groom and their home, Thornfield Hall, in ruins.

In our text, it seems, the fear-fulfilment dream eventually turns into a wish-fulfilment one. At first, however, things are not good. The references to night and to her being in bed probably imply that. There is a spiritual gloom and, at first, a sense of false security in it.

Nevertheless, throughout these verses the beloved speaks of **'the one my heart** [or soul] **loves'** (see 3:1-4). It is the same phrase she used back in 1:7, where it was translated 'you whom I love'. This is the only other place where she employs this potent phrase. As is usually the case when the Bible uses the word 'heart' or 'soul', the idea is not that this is an entirely spiritual affection, but rather that it is thorough and entire, a heartfelt and deep-seated love. Despite her condition, her love for him is singular and sincere. This is what fuels her distress. Think of a ragged orphan lost in Manila and a well-dressed, much-loved child lost in Manchester. Both are in danger but the latter may well feel it more keenly, as five minutes earlier she was holding her mother's hand and all was well.

This raises the question for all of us: whom do you love from your heart — not only on the horizontal level but also, more importantly, on the vertical level? Do you love Jesus Christ from your heart? Is your soul devoted to him? That is how it should be if we are Christians. We should have ardent desires for him, fervent longings for his presence. How that affects your dream life is not so important. How it affects your waking life is very important indeed.

What happens here is that although 'all night long' the beloved looks 'for the one' her 'heart loves', she has to say, **'I looked for him but did not find him.'**

Firstly, note *the intensity of her love*. She has to find him now. She cannot go back to sleep, as it were, and resume her search in the morning. She has to find him right away. She brooks no delay.

Secondly, *her search is fruitless*. She longs to see him, but she cannot. She hunts high and low for him, but he is nowhere to be found. He has gone.

It may be a dream but it brings out very vividly what it means to lose one whom you truly love.

On the horizontal level first, think of broken engagements (which may sometimes be the right course of action but are never desirable) or, worse, families torn apart by divorce or death. We should have the deepest sympathy for anyone in such a position.

But then, on the vertical or spiritual plane, think of what it is like to go through a period of apparent spiritual desertion. Here is a truly converted believer. He reads the Word, but it does not seem to come home to him as it once did. He prays, but he feels as though his prayers go no higher than the ceiling. He is not getting through. A thick duvet seems to envelop his soul. Such a person will usually still come to church, but there seems to be a deadness on him. It is not like it once was:

> O LORD, when you favoured me,
>   you made my mountain stand firm;
> but when you hid your face,
>   I was dismayed
>
> (Ps. 30:7).

That sort of experience can come to a believer. It happens for various reasons. It is sometimes referred to as the 'dark night of the soul', an idea that has its roots in mysticism. Protestant writers usually prefer the term 'spiritual desertion'. It does not mean that such a person has lost his salvation, or is no longer in union with Christ, but that he loses the joy of salvation and the reality of communion. Fellowship founders; communication crumbles. My interface with heaven crashes. It produces thoughts such as those expressed in these well-known words penned in the eighteenth century by William Cowper, a man who knew something about spiritual melancholy:

Where is the blessedness I knew
When first I saw the Lord?
Where is the soul-refreshing view
Of Jesus and his Word?

What peaceful hours I once enjoyed!
How sweet their memory still!
But now I feel an aching void,
The world can never fill.

It is similar to what the psalmist describes in Psalms 42-44. Especially note the following passage:

I say to God my Rock,
　Why have you forgotten me?
Why must I go about mourning,
　oppressed by the enemy?
My bones suffer mortal agony
　as my foes taunt me,
saying to me all day long,
　'Where is your God?'
Why are you downcast, O my soul?
　Why so disturbed within me?

(Ps. 42:9-11).

In Psalm 44:23-24 we see a corporate experience of this.

Do you know something of this distressing experience? It happens to believers, just as it happened to this woman. A passage like this is here to show us what to do in such a situation.

The testing experience of seeking a lover lost

Because of this situation the beloved decides to do something. Throughout the dream she is very practical, very earnest. She decides on a careful, thorough, painstaking and methodical search for him. She says:

> **I will get up now and go about the city,**
> **through its streets and squares;**
> **I will search for the one my heart loves**

> (3:2).

In the light of the reference to the city, which, as we have already seen, is perhaps figuratively and poetically less in tune with the themes of love and romance than the countryside, we remember that there are hostile forces at work determined to undermine intimate relationships such as this one. This is partly borne out by verse 3.

Nevertheless, she is determined to find him, regardless of danger. It is a little like the question and answer in Psalm 42:11:

> Why are you downcast, O my soul?
>   Why so disturbed within me?
> Put your hope in God,
>   for I will yet praise him,
>   my Saviour and my God.

The same sort of attitude ought to be there for any of us when it comes to the loss of a lover.

Firstly, on the horizontal level, obviously where a situation is beyond repair — for example, when a partner has died — this verse cannot be applied directly, although in many such cases there is much to be said for remarriage, and maybe that is an application. There are many other situations where things are in the balance. You look like losing the one your heart loves. Do not sit back and let it happen. Be up and doing what you can to win that person back, to save the marriage. Where did things start to go wrong? Are there sins to repent of? How can matters be put right? Look for help. Similar things could be said about a breakdown in any relationship. Go and seek the sheep that is lost, and bring it home.

On the vertical plane, the approach is similar. When we feel deserted by Jesus it is often because we first deserted him. We need to retrace our steps and consider where things began to go wrong. Remember Abraham's disastrous time in Egypt and how he eventually returned to Bethel, to the place where he had been before, where he had worshipped God with sacrifices. There he once again called on the name of the Lord. We must be determined to meet with Christ and find communion with him afresh. It is a matter for earnestness, thoroughness and great effort on our part, until the situation is resolved. This is true individually and corporately. We must do all we can.

She goes on, however: **'So I looked for him but did not find him'** (3:2). Again we see the immediacy, the insistence, the impulsiveness, the impetuosity. Yet how disappointing! How distressing and discouraging! What frustration! She looks everywhere — in the open squares and on the main roads, along the thoroughfares and major highways, in the back streets and side streets, in alleyways and lanes, in holes and ditches. But he is nowhere to be found. He has seemingly vanished. He has disappeared into thin air. She looks up and down; she searches every place; but he is not there.

We must not suppose reconciliation is ever easy. There are no guarantees on the horizontal level. Nor may we assume that Christ is always easily found, either. It is not a simple matter of finding the right church, attending the right conference, or reading the right book. There can be times in a believer's life when Christ seems very distant, when he

seems very far from us. True union with Christ can never be
severed, but there may be loss of fellowship. Communion
can be interrupted; the relationship can falter.

She tells us in 3:3 that, in her dream, **'The watchmen
found me as they made their rounds in the city.'** Ironi-
cally, in the process of seeking, she herself is found. People
are not supposed to be out on the streets at this time of night
and, although they do not deal roughly with her, as in 5:7,
the watchmen are about to challenge her. However, before
they can say anything, she blurts out her question: **'Have
you seen the one my heart loves?'** Durham puts it like this:
'This is the sore upon which she keeps her finger … the
wound she keeps bleeding, till he bind it up.'

Perhaps this helps us to see how anyone who is really
serious about finding communion with Christ again will
inevitably speak to others about it. Perhaps it is not stretching
the point too much to think especially of one's parents or
guardians, and of Christian ministers in particular — those
whose work it is to keep watch over the city of God (Isa. 52:8;
56:10). It is perhaps not an easy thing to talk freely about, but
if we really love the Lord we shall want to discuss it. We shall
speak about our loss in similar terms to those we find here.
Such leaders will, at times, raise the subject anyway.

Something similar could be said on the horizontal level.
Sometimes married or courting couples need counselling.
We should not be ashamed to seek such advice if it is
thought necessary. By going to counsellors I do not necessarily mean professionals (such as Relate), but going to good
Christians who can where necessary talk things through with
a couple — experienced couples who have weathered some
of the storms that inevitably come in even the most wonderful unions. It can be very helpful, especially for a younger
couple, to talk with an older couple about such difficulties. It
is certainly far better to resort to this than to see the whole
relationship slowly slide into an irredeemable oblivion.

The happy experience of finding a lover lost

Finally, in 3:4, we have the dénouement as she reveals: **'Scarcely had I passed them when I found the one my heart loves.'** Whether the guards helped or hindered her is unclear but, at last, she discovers him. Here he is! Archimedes leaping from his bath crying 'Eureka!' was not more jubilant! She is overjoyed:

> **I held him and would not let him go**
> **till I had brought him to my mother's house,**
> **to the room of the one who conceived me.**

She holds onto him like Jacob holding onto the angel at Peniel.

It is suggested that this verse acts as a sort of *inclusio* with 3:1, which has her at home on her bed (perhaps in her mother's room). She is rewarded with the presence of her lover once again, back in her childhood home. Even in her dream she anticipates the happy union that lies ahead. The location, **'my mother's house'**, suggests both intimacy and security. It is presumably both where she was conceived in love and where she grew up in safety.

What distress losing him had caused her! Now, having found him again, she takes hold of him and is understandably determined not to let him go. She hugs him. She clasps him to her. She hangs on to him. She is determined that he shall accompany her home. She will not let him out of her sight. Limpet-like, she resolutely clings on.

Spurgeon spells out three stages here. We can speak of the *euphoria* of finding him. This involves knowing his person and experiencing his presence. We can speak of the *ecstasy* of holding him, a deeper and more sustained experience again. We can speak, thirdly, of the *elation* of bringing

him to 'my mother's house', which Spurgeon applies to the
sharing of our experience with others.

Reconciliations do occur on the horizontal level. Love's
fires can be rekindled, drowsy devotion awoken, romance
revived. We should not automatically assume that all is lost
the moment things start going wrong. Pray for strong marriages in the churches and in society, locally and nationally.
Pray against all that would weaken the institution of marriage. Do nothing to undermine anyone's marriage in any
way — either your own or that of anyone else. When storms
come, do all you can to weather them and to help those who
need help to get back on track. Perhaps the woman's crucial
role here is a warning against stereotyping the female role in
such situations.

On the spiritual plane, too, reconciliations occur: 'Seek
and you will find.' Seasons of refreshing come; clouds pass;
lost paths are rediscovered; assurance is regained; hair grows
again and strength returns; sheep are found; sons return.
While on earth we always have the hope of better days
ahead, and beyond this world there lies one that will be
brighter yet. Sometimes we find Christ soon, sometimes late;
sometimes we find him in the midst of his people, sometimes
after a meeting, sometimes before. We must use all available
means to seek him, but we must not rest in any one of these
means as being infallible. Whenever we do find him, we
must hold on to him as best we can, determined never again
to let him go, but rather to bring him home, as it were, never
to depart again until the consummation of heaven.

A warning conclusion

What lows and highs this woman experienced! She had
descended into a deep and seemingly inescapable trough.
She had ascended again to the highest peak. Even if it was a

dream, it was in part something approaching a nightmare and she had been very involved emotionally — going down to the depths of sadness at her loss and rising to the heights of joy at finding her lover again. One modern writer says, 'Love not only brings a greater experience of joy but a deeper capacity for pain as well.' This is probably why, in 3:5, she repeats the warning previously found in 2:7:

> **Daughters of Jerusalem, I charge you**
> **by the gazelles and by the does of the field:**
> **Do not arouse or awaken love**
> **until it so desires.**

Love can be like the proverbial emotional roller coaster. As a popular singer put it, 'Love can mend your life, but love can break your heart.' We need to be prepared for its contrasting elevations and depressions, upturns and downturns. That is why, although it often happens, it is not ideal for adolescents in Western society to be preoccupied with such matters. Such young people are already facing many emotional upheavals and tests without introducing a further element. If a child can possibly get through his or her early to mid-teens without awakening or arousing love, then that is all to the good. Sadly, many are determined that this will not be the case and, through certain popular magazines aimed at young girls and by other means, they constantly pump out propaganda to say that if you are not busy falling in love then you are not really living the life of a teenager. We can all do without such misinformation.

One result of all this is that the average age for first-time sex in the UK is now down to sixteen years, the lowest age on record. As a consequence the incidence of sexually transmitted diseases among teenagers is rapidly rising and teenage pregnancies in Britain now occur in forty-two cases out of a thousand — all this on top of what can be a difficult emotional issue anyway. A level of emotional maturity is very desirable before we start thinking seriously about love and marriage. That means to say that we will take care both with our own feelings and with those of any whom we consider approaching on this level.

While we are considering a book that spends most of its time lauding marriage and sexual relations, it is important that we recall the many positive things that the Bible has to say about celibacy and chastity in general. In Matthew 19:12 Jesus observes that 'Some are eunuchs because they were born that way; others were made that way by men.' The reference seems to be both literal and metaphorical. Some are born physically unable to engage in sexual relations and some simply have a very low sex drive and so lack the inclination to marry. Especially in the East, keepers of royal harems were castrated. Others, though physically capable of marriage, are kept from it by various circumstances, such as caring for a bedridden relative. Jesus also speaks of some who, like himself, 'have renounced marriage [literally, 'made themselves eunuchs'] because of the kingdom of heaven'. The apostle Paul is perhaps the most outstanding example (although he may have been a widower rather than unmarried). Jesus says, 'The one who can accept this should accept it.'

On this matter, Richard Bewes helpfully reminds us in one of his books that chastity is not truncation (though trivializing sex is); innocence is not ignorance; want is not need, and permissiveness is not freedom. He quotes Richard Foster as saying, 'No one has yet died from a lack of sexual intercourse. Many have lived full and interesting lives without genital sex, including Jesus.'

It is good, too, for those who are young Christians, or who are not yet converted, to know that there are ups and downs in the Christian walk, griefs as well as joys, tragedies as well as triumphs. It is never a perfectly smooth walk to heaven. There are undulations. There are difficulties and setbacks.

We must expect these. The Bible speaks often enough of such things.

I mentioned Charlotte Brontë earlier. In the 1840s her sister Anne wrote these wise words:

Believe not those who say
The upward path is smooth,
Lest thou shouldst stumble in the way
And faint before the truth.

In his commentary, Tremper Longman III refers to Jack Lundborn's work. Like others before him, he has attempted to draw parallels between 3:1-4 and John 20:11-18, where Mary Magdalene comes to Jesus' tomb looking for him. Finding him gone, she asks two angels who are present where she might find him. Then, as she turns, Jesus himself confronts her. She takes him to be the gardener at first but then, realizing who he is, she holds on to him, just as the woman here in the Song of Songs does with her re-discovered lover. In John there is no 'coming to her mother's house', but there is the prospect of Mary going to be with him in *his* house. That is a good note on which to end this chapter. With regard to the risen Lord, life on earth is in many ways a series of sometimes frustrating seekings and searchings. As Bob Dylan once put it:

Sometimes I think I hear his voice;
Other times it's only me.

However, for believers, there is a world to come when all the hunting and questing will be at an end. He will welcome us in and dry all our tears. We shall hold on to him and he will hold on to us and there will be no letting go ever again. What a prospect is ours!

Goodness and mercy all my life
Shall surely follow me;
And in God's house for evermore
My dwelling place shall be.

Why? In the words of James G Small:

For I am his and he is mine
For ever and for ever.

To sum up

Where we know of a marriage, or a similar relationship, that
is in trouble, we ought to have the deepest sympathy. Some
situations are beyond repair, but never be too quick to write
off a relationship. When things are hanging in the balance
everything must be done to rescue the situation. Seek help if
necessary. What a boon good counselling can be! Reconciliations do occur. Pray for strong marriages. The path of
true love is seldom smooth; we must be ready for its highs
and its lows. A degree of emotional maturity is highly
desirable before we even begin on the road to love and
marriage.

There is such a thing as spiritual desertion. True union
with Christ can never end but, for various reasons, there may
be loss of fellowship. Finding a way out is not easy, but we
must be determined to meet with Christ and find communion
with him again. Reconciliation is often difficult. Anyone
who is in earnest about regaining communion with Christ
will speak to others about it, especially to Christian ministers. There is no easy way to heaven. We must expect difficulties. One comfort for us, though, is the prospect of never-
ending bliss in Christ's presence in the world to come. Think
often of it.

7.
Ceremony: Two lovers married — a wedding procession

Please read Song of Songs 3:6-11

Prospective brides often spend a good deal of time choosing the music to accompany their march up the aisle. Various things are used today, not just Mendelssohn or Mozart. There is an urban myth about a bride requesting the theme from the film *Robin Hood, Prince of Thieves*, Bryan Adams' apposite '[Everything I do] I do for you', but getting the rather less appropriate theme from *The Adventures of Robin Hood*, a 1960s ATV series all about Robin and his merry men.

We have no idea what music, if any, attended the proceedings here. A combination of 'Ride on, ride on in majesty', 'Thine be the glory' and 'Ye gates, lift up your heads' would perhaps have been fitting! Music or no music, we want to consider what is, once again, a relatively brief section, and learn from it.

As stated previously, the section deals, it would seem, with the marriage ceremony itself and beyond. The wedding day has a crucial place in the whole story. It is not the day when love began, or necessarily the most important day of the marriage, but it is a significant day, a noteworthy day, full of moment, a day that is celebrated and that is marked by a great deal of anticipation and excitement.

As we have seen, many rebel against such ideas, especially in our day. Cynicism towards marriage is common.
'Not a word but a sentence,' says a wit. 'Advice to persons
about to marry,' wrote another, '— don't'. 'Wedlock is a
padlock,' is a proverb; 'acrimony' (instead of 'matrimony')
and 'deadlock' are mischievous malapropisms, 'Married is
marred' a play on words. 'When you were engaged you felt
you could eat her; now you are married you wish you had,' is
another old quip. 'Who needs a bit of paper to make things
legitimate? Why bother with a marriage ceremony?' many
people say today.

In Alexander McCall Smith's third novel about 'The
No. 1 Ladies' Detective Agency', *Morality for beautiful
girls*, his heroine, Mma Ramotswe, reflects on how even in
Botswana there are many who take this attitude. She shows
some sympathy towards them but, as she says, although
marriage can offer no guarantee of permanence, 'At least
both people said they wanted a lifelong union. Even if they
proved to be wrong, at least they had tried.' She and her
friend Mma Makutsi lament the way married men so often
reach their forties and decide it is time to put in for a younger
model. What unhappiness such behaviour brings!

In the UK there are currently over 150,000 divorces every
year. There are areas of the country where over half the
children are born out of wedlock. The vulnerability of such
children is statistically very high. From every point of view,
marriage makes more sense than cohabitation. Simply
slipping into a live-in relationship is not a good idea and
often does not work for very long. Though the divorce rate is
high, there are many more failures when people simply live
together. There is evidence to say that, far from preparing
people for marriage, cohabitation makes an eventual break-
up more likely. A report in 2000 stated that 'Such marriages
are *twice as likely* to end in breakdown.' It is far better, far
wiser, to set a specific day when a public coming together

takes place, when formally and purposefully the marriage begins. As Mma Ramotswe acknowledges, this cannot, of course, secure anything in and of itself, but this is the right pattern set down for us in the Bible.

Despite the cynicism and fear, let us assert with Luther that 'There is no more lovely, friendly and charming relationship, communion or company than a good marriage.' As the English proverbs say, 'A faithful wife is the joy of life,' and 'As your wedding ring wears, so away go your cares.'

As we have noted, chapter 3 divides into two obvious parts, one coming before the wedding and one after it. Having considered 'a lover lost and found', we now turn to the subject of 'two lovers married', and their wedding ceremony in particular.

Again it is the woman who is probably the main speaker, with the initial question being asked by someone else, probably the daughters of Jerusalem.

Shulammite	Friends	Solomon
—	3:6	—
3:7-11	—	—

As Duane Garrett observes, 'Every young man in love is a "Solomon in all his glory"' but once again we shall put particular emphasis here on the vertical lessons — what the passage teaches us about a relationship with the Lord. Here are very useful lessons about the wedding procession that is the Christian life.

Some dispute the idea that 3:6-11 describes a wedding march, but I am convinced that this is a description of the marriage procession into Jerusalem, which is followed (in chapter 4) by festivities at the royal palace. Some argue that the dream sequence continues. Even if that is so, there is a definite break between verses 5 and 6.

We have all been to weddings. Have you ever been to a wedding involving people from a culture other than your own? Marriage customs differ according to the background of the people concerned. Many core elements are similar, but there is plenty of variation. Traditional Jewish weddings, usually large affairs, are quite different from, say, traditional Hindu ones, which tend to be even larger affairs. Asian brides are expected to look sad because they are leaving their parents behind. Hungarian couples often not only cut the cake but hand out slices to the guests. Greek couples like to arrive at the church together. At the reception when my wife's cousin married her American husband, a chink of champagne glasses from anywhere in the room required the happy couple to kiss and, after the cake was cut, they fed each other — not things I have come across in weddings where both partners were British.

The variations are endless. Most marriages, however, include a procession. That is what we have here. It is best to think in terms of a royal parade rather than what happens in traditional British weddings. It was common in that time and place for the bride and groom together, or sometimes separately, to proceed to the wedding place with pomp and circumstance. This seems to have been the norm anyway. It is also worth noting that, whereas at weddings today, at least in the West, all eyes are usually on the bride, here it is quite the opposite. All eyes are on the groom. There are three things in particular to observe.

A procession out of the desert and on to glory

In these verses either the woman or a crowd of onlookers speaks and describes Solomon and his entourage travelling along the road into Jerusalem from the desert. **'Desert'** means open and uncultivated country, wilderness, not necessarily barren land. From the walls of the city, perhaps, we look out, and what do we see? The question is asked in 3:6:

Who is this coming up from the desert
  like a column of smoke,
perfumed with myrrh and incense
  made from all the spices of the merchant?

Our curiosity is aroused. We are inquisitive. It reminds us of the question asked when Jesus entered Jerusalem in that last week before his death, 'Who is this?' (Matt. 21:10), and also of Peter's statement that angels long to look into the things concerning salvation (1 Peter 1:12).

It is not clear at first who is coming, although a female is expected. It soon becomes apparent what this pageant is. John Flavel speaks of spectators invited and a spectacle beheld. It is reminiscent of a caravan of merchants (the word **'merchant'** is found here), as in Genesis 37:25, when the sons of Israel 'looked up and saw a caravan of Ishmaelites coming from Gilead. Their camels were loaded with spices, balm and myrrh.' Or think of the arrival in Jerusalem of the Queen of Sheba, 'with a very great caravan — with camels carrying spices', as well as gold and jewels, as she came to Solomon to talk with him about all she had on her mind. 'Never again were so many spices brought in as those the queen of Sheba gave to King Solomon' (1 Kings 10:2,10).

Here it is the groom who draws near. Some disagree, but in my opinion the bride is already with him. A great pillar of smoke is rising at the head of the column. All sorts of pungent spices and incense burn in the air and will soon be scenting the atmosphere. What a beautiful aroma perfumes the area all around the parade! This was frequently done in such processions but there is something unique about this occasion.

Scripture has positive things to say about being single and will not allow us to disparage that state. It is a good gift from God. However, the Bible is also very positive about marriage and it is acceptable to see marriage ideally as leaving behind a desert and entering into a most desirable state, symbolized here by the perfume of myrrh and incense. It is, as John Newton declared, when the 'parties are united by affection, and the general conduct is governed by religion and prudence ... not only an honourable but a comfortable state'. This is why a wedding ceremony, for all the tears some may shed, should be a time of celebration and joy.

The pillar of smoke reminds us of God's presence with his people in the desert. Indeed, the description is an obvious echo of the Israelites' approach to Canaan. Remember how, 'By day the LORD went ahead of them in a pillar of cloud to guide them on their way and by night in a pillar of fire to give them light, so that they could travel by day or night. Neither the pillar of cloud by day nor the pillar of fire by night left its place in front of the people' (Exod.13:21-22).

Perhaps Spurgeon is right to see the pillars of smoke as indicating burning lamps — that certainly fits in with the wedding custom we know of in connection with Jesus' parable of the ten virgins. If smoke suggests God's presence, light does so even more. God is light, and Jesus is the Light of the world. His disciples are too and, as Spurgeon observes, 'the thick smoke of her suffering' accompanies the church all the way.

Such sacrifices are a sweet-smelling aroma to God. The various perfumes and fragrances mentioned here speak of God's glory too. In the temple there was a golden altar of incense on which every morning and evening the high priest was to burn a specially concocted and exclusive mixture, including frankincense, galbanum and onycha. This sacred act was an integral part of temple worship. Certain sacrifices on the bronze altar were also to have incense added to them.

At its dedication, among the gifts brought to the tabernacle by the twelve tribes were twelve golden dishes of incense.

Myrrh was, of course, one of the gifts that the Magi, or Wise Men, offered to Jesus while he was still an infant. Such a gift has traditionally been understood as speaking of Christ's divine nature. It 'owns a deity nigh'.

More than once a parallel is drawn in Scripture between prayer and the offering of incense to God. For example, in Psalm 141:2 the writer says, 'May my prayer be set before you like incense; may the lifting up of my hands be like the evening sacrifice' (see also Rev. 8:3).

In 2 Corinthians 2 Paul speaks of preaching the gospel using this imagery. He describes his missionary work in terms of a triumphal march into the city like that of a conquering hero. He describes it as always being led 'in triumphal procession in Christ'. It is spreading 'everywhere the fragrance of the knowledge of him. For we are to God the aroma of Christ among those who are being saved and those who are perishing. To the one we are the smell of death; to the other, the fragrance of life.' He is thinking of the heady aroma that would hang over such a Roman triumph, following a great victory. The church in Christ both petitions and proclaims; it is prayerful and proselytizing.

Here, then, we see a picture of Christ bringing his pleading and prophetic church, which so longs for a better country, out of the wilderness of this world. With Spurgeon and others, I see this passage as describing 'the progress of the hidden Christ through the world' and 'his true church ... also hidden ...', but together 'carried through the world in the sumptuous chariot' described here. Christ is bringing his people into the glory of heaven above, the New Jerusalem, and the marriage supper of the Lamb, which is to come. I have a friend in South Africa, a pastor, who heads his regular prayer letters with the words: 'En route to glory'. That is how we ought to think of our lives here as Christians, going on from glory to glory in a wedding procession.

> We're marching through Immanuel's ground
> To fairer worlds on high.

Or, to quote another hymn:

> We are marching home to God
> In the way our fathers trod.

A procession that focuses on the groom

The questioner seems to be expecting a bride, or at least a woman, but that is not where the focus of the passage actually is. The question of 3:6 is answered in 3:7-8. Perhaps it is others who speak but, following the NIV, we shall assume that it is in fact the beloved. She says:

> **Look! It is Solomon's carriage,**
> **escorted by sixty warriors,**
> **the noblest of Israel,**
> **all of them wearing the sword,**
> **all experienced in battle,**
> **each with his sword at his side,**
> **prepared for the terrors of the night.**

More literally, the opening phrase is: 'Look! Solomon's bed.' The context suggests, however, something more like a couch, coach or carriage. This is the royal bed-cum-chariot, that of Solomon the king! If we were in any doubt at all, every uncertainty is dispelled now. It is surrounded by Solomon's choicest band of warriors, his palace guard. They number some sixty in all, twice the number of David's mighty men (as recorded in 2 Sam. 23) — 'a competent and sufficient number' says Durham. (Later, in 6:8, we also read of sixty queens.) In Psalm 45 it is the king himself who bears the sword and scatters his enemies with arrows. It all speaks of power and prestige, wealth and honour. The soldiers are wearing their swords, chiefly for ceremonial reasons today, but they are experienced fighters and no one dare attack by day or by night. Like the guards outside Buckingham Palace, they are there not only as a guard of honour but also to protect their charge. This is not an empty display of nobility and prowess. These men are well able to defend the royal couple from any and every danger, whether it comes by day or by night.

The duty to protect his wife is an important part of a husband's calling. He is to be considerate and respectful and care for her 'as the weaker partner' (1 Peter 3:7). He may not have sixty warriors on hand to guard her, but he prays that the angels of heaven will watch over her at all times and he does all he can to shield and shelter her from every hurt or harm. Husbands, do you care for your wives as you should?

The armed men remind us of the angels, of whom the Saviour said that one word to his Father would bring 'more than twelve legions' to help him (Matt. 26:53). They serve the heirs of salvation and are able to oppose the forces of darkness. Even though we are believers, there are nights of darkness and temptation, yet none need fear 'the terror of night, nor the arrow that flies by day, nor the pestilence that stalks in the darkness, nor the plague that destroys at mid-day'. Why not?

> For he will command his angels concerning you
>   to guard you in all your ways;
> they will lift you up in their hands,
>   so that you will not strike your foot against a stone
>   (Ps. 91:5-6,11-12).

Scripture tells us the angels are ready at Christ's command to do his will at any time. This reminds us that God's people are safe as they travel to the marriage supper. They have a safe conduct that cannot be violated. Durham rightly says, 'There is no king or monarch so well attended and guarded, or who may sleep so secure and sound as a believer.' 'The angel of the LORD encamps around those who fear him, and he delivers them' (Ps. 34:7).

As the procession draws near, it can be seen more clearly, and so further details are given. The word used for **'carriage'** in 3:9 is found only here. It may be related to a Greek word meaning 'carriage' or 'pavilion'. Otherwise the context has to dictate the meaning, which suggests a litter or palanquin.

> **King Solomon made for himself the carriage;**
> **he made it of wood from Lebanon.**
> **Its posts he made of silver,**
> **its base of gold.**
> **Its seat was upholstered with purple,**
> **its interior lovingly inlaid**
> **by the daughters of Jerusalem**
>
> (3:9-10).

Solomon has made it, or at least designed it, himself of the best wood — probably cedar from Lebanon. Solomon was famous for importing cedar from Hiram, King of Tyre. It is a most durable wood. Several rare and technical terms are then used. It seems that the carriage has silver posts and a gold base. Inside, its seat has been lovingly upholstered, or upholstered in love, with rare and precious purple cloth with careful inlaid work all around — the work, it seems, of the daughters of Jerusalem. Only the finest materials are employed. Opulence and prosperity, luxury and magnificence are again hallmarks of the description, but love has an important place. How lovingly the daughters of Jerusalem have inlaid the interior — or, to follow the text more closely, 'with love it was inlaid'. Each succeeding item seems to be more precious — 'wood from Lebanon ... silver ... gold ... its interior with love inlaid'. 'The further in we come in the covenant,' says Durham, 'we will find it the more rich.'

A man must make thorough preparations for his bride if he is to be a Christ-like husband. He must provide for her the best that he can. Circumstances may dictate a limited budget and so he may be able to provide only the basics in material terms. However, he should make the best of what he has, providing what is both beautiful and durable. At all times love must motivate and permeate all that he does.

We have already thought of the temple. The materials listed here — wood from Lebanon, posts and bases of silver and gold, purple cloth, intricate inlay work — all remind us of the temple too. The idea of its being carried through the desert speaks especially of the tabernacle. Perhaps we think chiefly of the ark of the covenant, a potent symbol of the presence of God, being carried by the priests up from the desert.

Here, then, is something more of the glory of the Christian life. In regard to sumptuousness and splendour and also to comfort and care, God amply provides for his people. He has, as it were, made a splendid carriage for them and in it he carries them all the way to glory. They respond in love and affectionately adore him, as do the daughters of Jerusalem. Do we appreciate enough what a glorious thing God has done in providing the means of salvation? Are we sufficiently aware what a grand thing it is to be borne aloft in God's carriage? Are we suitably conscious with regard to how comfortable the way to heaven really is in Christ? It is all the work of the one greater than Solomon, the Lord Jesus Christ himself.

A procession that culminates in a day of crowning and joy

Finally, the procession arrives in Jerusalem and the shout goes up:

> **Come out, you daughters of Zion,**
> **and look at King Solomon wearing the crown,**
> **the crown with which his mother crowned him**
> **on the day of his wedding,**
> **the day his heart rejoiced**
>
> (3:11).

The phrase **'daughters of Zion'** is found only here. It is an alternative to the expression 'daughters of Jerusalem' that was used in the previous verse. **'Zion'** refers to the heart of Jerusalem.

The bride is not mentioned. Her description comes later, in chapter 4. All eyes are now on the king.

There are applications here on the horizontal level, of course. Male headship is clearly implied. Hebrews 13:4 reminds us that 'Marriage should be honoured by all, and the marriage bed kept pure, for God will judge the adulterer and all the sexually immoral.' The joy of Christian marriage is also evident. As has already been stated, a wedding should be a happy occasion and should presage a lifetime of contentment. Having said that, as we draw towards the close of this chapter, I want us to concentrate especially on Christ.

This is **'the day his heart rejoiced'**. It was 'for the joy set before him' that Christ 'endured the cross, scorning its shame, and sat down at the right hand of the throne of God' (Heb. 12:2). Even greater joy lies ahead, when he will declare: 'Here am I, and the children God has given me' (Heb. 2:13; see Isa. 8:18). 'As a bridegroom rejoices over his bride, so will your God rejoice over you' (Isa. 62:5).

John tells us how he heard in heaven 'what sounded like a great multitude, like the roar of rushing waters and like loud peals of thunder, shouting:

"Hallelujah!
　For our LORD God Almighty reigns.
Let us rejoice and be glad
　and give him glory!
For the wedding of the Lamb has come,
　and his bride has made herself ready"'
(Rev. 19:6-7).

Every eye gazes at the king. He wears what may be a crown used for this special occasion or, more likely, it is the royal crown. There is nothing to compare with it. It is fascinating that it is the king's mother who puts the crown on his head. In Solomon's own lifetime it would have been Bathsheba who did this. What does the term **'mother'** point to when we attempt to think of Christ? Surely not to Mary, his mother in the physical sense. Rather, it points to all those who do his will — the church, his people. Remember Jesus' own words in Luke 8:21: 'My mother and brothers are those who hear God's word and put it into practice.' Moreover, we are Christ's mother in the sense that he is formed in us (Gal. 4:19).

The bride here would also one day place a crown on her son's head. We who together are the bride of Christ are the ones who must obey Christ now and who will give him the glory in the world to come. Christ is King by virtue of his deity, his being the one mediator between God and man and his kingly office as the Christ. Flavel argues that when we were converted we crowned Christ as King over our souls. When a king is crowned he is given the right to reign. It is a glorious day when people gladly consent to his reigning and a day of great gladness and joy. All these things and more can be applied to conversion. Of course, in other respects there are differences — in Christ there is no dissension, no death, no degeneration into tyranny, and a delight known not only here on earth but also in heaven above.

There is, further, a crowning day that, to quote some well-known hymns, is 'coming by and by', when believers will 'crown him with many crowns, the Lamb upon his throne'. Then will 'crowns of glory ever bright rest upon the Victor's head', a royal diadem will adorn 'the mighty Victor's brow'. They will 'bring forth the royal diadem to crown him Lord of all'. We shall sing, suggests Thomas Kelly, 'Mighty Victor, reign for ever; wear the crown so dearly won,' and on bended knee all will 'confess him King of glory now'. On earth his only crown was made of thorns ('Ne'er forget the wormwood and the gall'), but in heaven we shall see him seated on a white cloud, the one who is 'like a son of man'. He will have 'a crown of gold on his head and a sharp sickle in his hand' (Rev. 14:14). Indeed, 'on his head' there will be 'many crowns' (Rev. 19:12). What a day of unmitigated joy that will be for all who are his! We should think of it often.

Meanwhile we ought to look forward to that day, seeking to give all the glory to him even now. 'Crown him as your Captain in temptation's hour,' is Caroline Noel's pithy phrase. Watts prays, 'Let every act of worship be like our espousals, Lord, to thee.' As someone once put it, before conversion we put the crown on our own heads; after conversion we put it on Christ's head. We should crown him daily, in the words of Bridges and Thring, as Lord of life, love, peace and years ('the Potentate of time').

> Awake my soul and sing
> Of him who died for thee,
> And hail him as thy matchless King
> Through all eternity.

To sum up

Marriage is a very positive thing — a leaving behind of the desert. What a pleasure to be married!

A husband has a duty to provide for his wife and to protect her. Matthew Henry is often quoted as commenting on woman's creation and the fact that she was not made from the man's head to top him, nor from his feet to be trampled on, 'but out of his side to be equal with him, under his arm to be protected and near his heart to be loved'.

Here we see Christ bringing his church out of the desert of this world into the glory of heaven above and the marriage supper of the Lamb. As Christians we should think of our lives here as a wedding procession, leading on from glory to glory.

In regard to splendour and to comfort, God amply provides for us. He carries us all the way. The appropriate response is love and adoration.

We who together form Christ's bride must obey him now, knowing that we shall give him all glory in the world to come. 'The crowning day is coming by and by,' when believers will 'crown him with many crowns, the Lamb upon his throne'. What a day of unalloyed delight that will be!

8.
Consummation
Praising, wooing and loving

Please read Song of Songs 4:1 – 5:1

The word 'consummation' means 'climax, completion or culmination'. We use it in particular to refer to sexual union within marriage. After the wedding, and not before, comes the consummation, the time of full physical union between bride and groom.

King Henry VIII's first wife was Catherine of Aragon. She believed, in opposition to Henry's own eventual view, that her previous marriage, to Henry's deceased brother Arthur, had been rightly annulled because the marriage was never consummated. Henry's third marriage, to Anne of Cleves, was annulled on grounds of non-consummation. In English law today a marriage can be declared void if it can be reasonably determined that it is unconsummated. Still today you may hear that a marriage 'was not consummated' or 'was unconsummated'.

It would be unsafe just to assume that this is necessarily in line with a biblical understanding of marriage. Matthew 1:19 tells us that 'Because Joseph [Mary's] husband was a righteous man and did not want to expose her to public disgrace, he had in mind to divorce her quietly.' The word 'divorce' is used, even though it was a betrothal, not a marriage as such and, despite appearances, there had certainly been no consummation. On the other hand, the instinct to give a high place to consummation is surely correct. Verses such as Exodus 22:16 and Deuteronomy 22:29 appear to suggest this.

So far we have looked at the courtship between the lover and his beloved, described from the beginning up to 3:5, and then the wedding procession of the bridal couple, which comes in the second half of chapter 3. Now we shall consider 4:1 – 5:1, where we come, logically enough, to the very intimate matter of the consummation of love and to the real heart of the book.

In chapter 3 the focus is on the groom, on Solomon in all his glory. Here the focus switches to the bride, although, paradoxically, nearly every verse of this section is spoken by the groom. He is in fact more prominent as a speaker here than anywhere else in the book. The wedding ceremony is over. All the commotion of the day is complete. At last the bride and groom are alone together. At this point the door would normally be closed and what happened next would be entirely unobserved by any third party. Even in some parts of the Middle East, where to this day there is something of a ceremony involving the production of a cloth to prove virginity and so on, this is still very much a personal and private moment.

The story is told of the fanatical disciple of a certain Jewish rabbi who was so keen to learn everything he could from his teacher that he even wanted first-hand knowledge of how to conduct himself in the marriage bed. In order to do this he hid himself in his master's bedroom at a time when he knew that the rabbi and his wife would be retiring for the night. Fortunately, he was discovered before he could gain any knowledge of his teacher's bedroom technique and was quite correctly thrown out without ceremony. Here, however, things are different and we are allowed to

follow this special couple into the bridal suite itself and
discover at least something of what happens next. So we
come at last to love's consummation.

The pattern is as follows:

Shulammite	Friends	Solomon
—	—	4:1-15
4:16	—	—
—	—	5:1a,b
—	5:1c	—

The groom praises his bride

First, we have a song of matchless beauty sung by Solomon
the king to his virgin bride, the Shulammite, in 4:1-7. He
praises her in ways that we might not always immediately
appreciate, but that are similar to Eastern traditions such as
the Syrian *wasf*, documented by Wetzstein and published by
biblical scholar Franz Delitzsch in the nineteenth century.
The *wasf* is apparently still sung at traditional weddings
today. Longman says this passage is the first of four *wasfs*
(5:10-16 describes the man; 6:4-6 and 7:1-9a are both about
the woman).

I recall listening, as a teenager, to Marc Bolan's 'Get it
on'. It includes lines such as 'You've got the teeth of the
hydra upon you,' and 'You're built like a car, oh yeah,'
intended compliments which could easily be misconstrued.
We have a similar type of problem here. Glickman describes discussing these verses with a friend on an aero-
plane. The friend thought he would try complimenting a
stewardess in this fashion. 'Your hair is like a flock of goats
descending from Mount Gilead,' he said to her. She was not
impressed! In its search for humour, the satirical magazine

The Wittenberg Door once used this passage as the basis for a grotesquely comical drawing depicting this poor woman.

Clearly literalists need to beware. At least one commentary ends up claiming that this is a description of an ugly country bumpkin because of its refusal to work with the metaphors. It is also worth bearing in mind that these metaphors are often important as much for their associations as for the images that they employ.

We should understand the passage, on the horizontal plane, as a lesson in how a man should appreciate his wife. When Jonathan Edwards first fell for his life's companion Sarah, he noted that 'When we behold a beautiful body, a lovely proportion, a beautiful harmony of features of face, delightful airs of countenance, and voice, and sweet motion and gesture; we are charmed with it.' This whole section also has something to teach us about how to approach wooing and even foreplay within marriage. We shall not discuss such matters in any detail, but if you are wise enough to take a hint you will see what the chapter contains and, where appropriate, will find abundant help in the right direction.

Commenting on this chapter, Dianne Bergant notes how 'People today are quite critical of any exaggerated concentration on female beauty,' especially if they feel it is reinforcing 'biased stereo-types', or minimizing other dimensions of womanhood. They want women to be valued for themselves, not just for their ability to boost the male ego, or make a man happy. However, as she notes, there is something enviably independent about this woman. She is neither coquettish nor cowed here.

On the vertical level, this passage speaks of the beauty of the church, a comeliness that is seen already here on earth in embryo form and that is going to be fully revealed at the end of time, when the Lord Christ comes again to take his people to himself.

1. Where the groom focuses his thoughts

The groom begins by saying, **'How beautiful you are, my darling! Oh, how beautiful!'** (4:1). He actually begins with a 'Lo' or 'Behold'. Perhaps 'Wow!' would be the dynamic equivalent, or another 'Oh' to match the one the NIV includes in the second sentence.

This is how a man ought to think of his wife. Obviously the attraction will be physical at first, but as he gets to know her, if she is what she should be, he will see that she also has inner beauty — 'the unfading beauty of a gentle and quiet spirit' (1 Peter 3:4). Where he does not see that, he will do what he can to nurture and to cultivate it. He will love his wife until she is radiant and unblemished in his eyes. He will cherish her and care for her as much as he cares for his own body. Husbands, are you loving your wives like that? Are they growing more beautiful as you grow in your love for them — not necessarily outwardly, but certainly inwardly?

In Sonnet 104 Shakespeare wrote:

To me, fair friend, you never can be old.
For as you were when first your eye I eyed,
Such seems your beauty still.

Our model should be Christ and his love for his people.

2. How the groom describes his bride

After looking at her face, Solomon goes on to list his bride's attributes, one by one. At this stage, it would seem the woman still has a veil over her face, which the man is about to remove. First, however, he takes in the sight. A veil serves both to hide beauty and to heighten desire. He focuses on seven things, seven being a number of completeness. In the first three images the metaphor follows the reference to a part of her face; in the second three the metaphor precedes it. Finally, he reverts to the initial order as he refers to her breasts. It is all very sensuous. The first thing that we need to do is to clarify the meaning of what is said and then make some applications.

Her eyes

'Your eyes behind your veil', he says, **'are doves'** (4:1). She apparently remains covered, but he is now close enough to see her face through the diaphanous gauze of the wedding veil. As she had likened his eyes to doves, so he now uses the same metaphor. The same idea appears back in 1:15. Mascara, eyeshadow, coloured lenses and other aids are often used to enhance the eyes — the brows, the lashes, the lids, the pupils. This woman did not need any of these. God had given her gentle, innocent, trusting eyes, redolent of her character. Is this your character too?

Her hair

'Your hair is like a flock of goats descending from Mount Gilead' (4:1). He looks next at her black hair, which is long and perhaps at this very moment is being untied so that it can cascade down on to her shoulders. The word for **'descending'** means something like 'flowing' or 'cascading'. There are no stray grey hairs here; no need of colourings, dyes, rinses or tints. Her hair is not lank or lifeless either, but has an attractive dark sheen. It reminds the groom of a flock of black goats coming down the mountain in the picturesque region of Gilead, east of the Jordan. Probably we should think of seeing the animals from a distance, across the valley, with the flock separating and running both to the left and to the right.

Human beings have an average of five million hairs on their bodies, 100 to 150 thousand of them on the head, all known to God. To be scientifically prosaic, this hair is dead protein. However, its poetic symbolism is rich and varied. In 1 Corinthians 11:15 Paul speaks of a woman's long hair as 'her glory'. It is given to her, he says, 'as a covering'. In Scripture a loss of hair is a sign of mourning and shame (Ezra 9:3; Isa. 3:17,24; 7:20; 15:2; 22:12; Jer. 7:29; 47:5; Amos 8:10) or of dedication (Num. 6:5). The anointing of the hair on the head speaks of abundance, joy and peace. Vivacity, joy and glory marked this woman, then — things that are plentifully found in Christ. Does that describe your life?

Her teeth

Your teeth are like a flock of sheep just shorn,
    coming up from the washing.
Each has its twin;
    not one of them is alone

(4:2).

The Hebrew includes alliteration. Someone once asked why missing teeth can look so charming in little children and yet so ugly in adults. Thanks to modern dentistry we do not see so many adults with missing teeth these days. There was a time when it was more common. It is said that this is why you rarely see people smiling in early photographs. People were not more morose then; they just knew that a smile would not be very attractive! This woman has no such problem. She did not have crooked teeth either, or an over-crowded mouth. Buck teeth, misaligned teeth, lower teeth that protruded, or wide gaps between her teeth, were not in evidence. Way before the advent of the orthodontist, she was showing the world the sort of smile that today's American teenager in braces longs for and dreams of. Either top matches bottom like the lambs and their reflection in the water, or each tooth on one side is matched by another, identical one, on the other side. Again using a rustic image, he says that they are like sheep just shorn and washed clean. They glisten white. The very image is designed to provoke a smile — which on her, of course, looked charming. It speaks also of the purity, the innocence and freshness which charac- terized her. She was radiant; she sparkled. Her beaming smile summed up her sunny, cheerful attitude. Do you share these latter characteristics?

Her lips

'Your lips are like a scarlet ribbon; your mouth is lovely' (4:3). The lips are the two fleshy folds that surround the mouth, or as Henry Gray accurately but prosaically put it in his famous *Anatomy*, they are 'fleshy folds which surround the *rima* or orifice of the mouth formed externally of integu- ment and internally of mucous membrane, between which are found the *Orbicularis oris* muscle, the labial vessels, some nerves, areolar tissue, and fat and numerous small labial glands'. One humorist put it this way: 'Lips are what's there to stop your mouth fraying.'

They tend to be redder than the rest of the face and it is generally accepted that their redness, fulness and shapeliness can be attractive. Female lips swell and become a deeper red with sexual arousal. According to one website, 'Full, lus- cious lips have always been sought after, regardless of age. A plump pout is considered to be a sign of youth and an icon of sensuality... We are mesmerized by their scarlet hue and caressed by their silky softness. The eyes may be the win- dows to the soul but the lips are definitely the gateway to sensuality.' They quote Shakespeare's *Romeo and Juliet*, which refers to the lips as 'two blushing pilgrims'.

Nobody wants dry, chapped or peeling lips. Their thin-
ning is one of many unwelcome changes that occur as we
grow older. In ancient times women used vegetable dyes to
colour their lips. Cleopatra famously used carmine and
henna. Victorian women would kiss rose-coloured crepe
paper. Today millions are spent annually on lipstick, lip-
gloss, lip-liner and similar cosmetics. This is why some
women pay good money to have collagen or other tissue
injected into their lips, or even undergo surgery for implants.
Our heroine again needs no such help. The groom declares
that her lips look like a scarlet ribbon. Her mouth looks
lovely. It is as red as a scarlet ribbon and as shapely as a
perfectly tied bow. The lips are also 'organs of speech
essential to certain articulations' and the unusual word for
'lips' used here is formed from the verb 'to speak'. No doubt
her mouth not only looked attractive but spoke honestly,
kindly and winningly. Does yours?

The sides of her face

**'Your temples behind your veil are like the halves of a
pomegranate'** (4:3). By her **'temples'** he probably means
her cheeks as well. Like other fruits, pomegranates are often
associated with romance in ancient literature and are an
obvious symbol of fertility. Here he thinks of one that has
been cut in two to reveal a red interior. She is healthy and
full of colour, without the aid of rouge, or blusher, or any
other cosmetic. Even through the veil he can see that. She
has the blush of innocence, the ruddiness of health, the glow
of vigour and the pink bloom of youth. Again life and vigour
are implied. How do I compare?

Her neck

Your neck is like the tower of David,
    built with elegance;
on it hang a thousand shields,
    all of them shields of warriors

(4:4).

The neck is another area that can make us look less than beautiful. Even if, unlike some of us, you have a long and elegant one, loose skin, wrinkles and an excess of fatty tissue can take away its smoothness and attractiveness. A double chin, sagging jowls and a 'chicken neck' are all unappealing. Apart from heredity and ageing, poor diet and posture often contribute to the muscles becoming flabby and withered.

We do not know where the Tower of David was, but it was clearly a tall, straight, elegantly built tower where shields would be hung. (Solomon has sixty warriors around him, but she has a thousand.) He compares her neck to it — long, slender and elegant, and decorated with a necklace of silver or gold discs. He is thinking of her deportment, her bearing, and the way that points to her upright and noble character. She was erect, straight, upstanding. Is your disposition similar?

Her cleavage

Your two breasts are like two fawns,
    like twin fawns of a gazelle
    that browse among the lilies

(4:5).

Below her neck he can see her cleavage, her chest. This is not something we would normally speak about perhaps, but we remember that the two are alone and about to consummate their marriage. The description deliberately stops after this (although verses 6-7 and 12-14 could be seen as further, more oblique, references to her physical appearance). He does not mean, of course, that her cleavage looked just like two four-legged fawns. Rather he is thinking of the gentleness, the softness of the down of baby deer, lying with their legs tucked underneath their bodies and their heads in the lilies. Softness, gentleness and a tender attitude are again implied, and we are prompted to ask of ourselves, do we share such qualities?

This, then, is how a man should look at his wife. He should love to look at her face. She should be beautiful to him. This is right and proper. It is interesting that this is where the focus is — not on her body, but on her face. That is right and noble. Of course, it would be superficial to think that Solomon was concerned only with outward beauty. Everything else we read in the Bible warns us against such an assumption and that is why I have sought to make the applications I have. We may not have pretty, good-looking faces, but what matters most is whether we are lovely on the inside and attractive in the way that we live.

The passage also teaches us how it will be in the world to come and how it already is now in part. Paul speaks of Christ giving himself up for the church to make her holy, 'cleansing her by the washing with water through the word', in order to 'present her to himself as a radiant church, without stain or wrinkle or any other blemish, but holy and blameless' (Eph. 5:26,27).

This is the work that is going on now, the beautifying work that is necessary in order to prepare us for that great day. We are like Queen Esther, undergoing a series of beauty treatments prior to the day when we shall go in to meet the King. He is working to sanctify us so that we are those who are pure and innocent, with a single eye for his glory, mouths

that declare his glory, upright and solid, yet tender and gentle
in his service. We are not there yet, but we shall be one day,
and then not only shall we gaze on Christ's beauty, but he
will also gaze on ours. Even now, 'The king is enthralled by
your beauty; honour him, for he is your lord' (Ps. 45:11).

> The LORD your God is with you,
>> he is mighty to save.
> He will take great delight in you,
>> he will quiet you with his love,
>> he will rejoice over you with singing
>
> (Zeph. 3:17).

2. What the groom desires to do

Next the man says:

> **Until the day breaks**
>> **and the shadows flee,**
> **I will go to the mountain of myrrh**
>> **and to the hill of incense.**
> **All beautiful you are, my darling;**
>> **there is no flaw in you**
>
> (4:6-7).

The opening phrase repeats 2:17. The anticipation is over;
now is the time for love's consummation. He pictures
himself entering a place in the evening, the time when the
fragrance from the hills is most intense. He wants to come in
and to see all her beauty, the sweet-smelling contours of her
gorgeous body. The reference to her being beautiful acts as
an *inclusio*, concluding the section which opened with the
similar reference in 4:1. She is physically flawless.

That is how a wedding night should be. In too many
instances young people have been so impatient that there is

no such wedding night. They spoil both the anticipation and the consummation. If you are still unmarried, do not make the mistake of forcing your way in too soon. Wait! If such an exhortation is too late, then turn from sin now and find forgiveness and a fresh start in Christ. Of course, we recognize that there are no physically flawless women. Not even the most beautiful woman goes so far as to think that she is perfect in every way, and most people appreciate the help that lighting, cosmetics and other helps can give. However, if we have eyes like this man's, we may look on a form of perfection.

And, to look higher, we see here a picture of the glories of heaven to come and the consummation there of love between Christ and his church. If we are those who truly trust in the Lord Jesus Christ we shall then know as we are now known; then we shall see him as he is and, not only that, but he will look on us and he will say, 'All beautiful you are, my darling; there is no flaw in you.'

Our beauty is often soiled and stained and spotted now. There are many flaws. But not then! Look forward to that great and glorious day as you put your faith in Christ.

The groom woos his bride

1. The groom calls to his bride

In 4:8-15 we have another poem, or pair of poems, from the groom. Once again the two are apart and he begins by calling her to come to him. He pictures her as being far away from Jerusalem — up in the bleak, snow-capped mountains of the far north, in places of potential danger and distress, where wild animals roam. The six-times repeated **'from'**, the references to four geographical locations and to two species of animal all add to the poetry. It can be seen as a call to

leave the world behind and to come to Christ, a descent that
is not easy but that will be safe if he is with us.

> **Come with me** [he says], **from Lebanon, my bride,**
> **come with me from Lebanon.**
> **Descend from the crest of Amana,**
> **from the top of Senir, the summit of Hermon,**
> **from the lions' dens**
> **and** [from] **the mountain haunts of the leopards**
>
> (4:8).

Isaac Watts applies it thus:

> He calls me from the leopard's den,
> From this wild world of beasts and men,
> To Zion, where his glories are;
> Not Lebanon is half so fair.
> Nor dens of prey, nor flowery plains,
> Nor earthly joys, nor earthly pains,
> Shall hold my feet or force my stay,
> When Christ invites my soul away.

We have had 'my darling', 'my beautiful one', 'my dove',
but here for the first time he calls her **'my bride'**, an epithet
he employs six times altogether, all within the confines of
this present section. In 4:9 he adds 'my sister', employed the
same number of times and within similar confines (the final
one is actually in 5:2). The term stresses closeness, familiarity and intimacy and is matched by what she says later in 8:1.

His call reminds us of the trumpet that will sound on the
Last Day and the way the angels will gather the elect from
the four corners of the world. Out of the mountains, caves
and holes in the ground they will stream, the saints of God.
All wandering and all danger will be over then. There will be
no more fear.

2. The groom is enchanted with his bride

Then he says:

> **You have stolen my heart, my sister, my bride;**
> **you have stolen my heart**
> **with one glance of your eyes,**
> **with one jewel of your necklace**

> (4:9).

The word **'my'** appears four times here, emphasizing their union. She is his sister-bride and she possesses his heart.

In Shakespeare's *As you like it*, Phoebe says to Silvius, 'Whoever loved, that loved not at first sight?' Is there such a thing as love at first sight? It is an interesting question. Many people believe in it and they will tell you the story of how they met their wife or husband, falling in love with them at first sight. In reality it is less romantic but probably more accurate to say that there is such a thing as attraction at first sight, an attraction that can lead very quickly to love — so quickly that we hardly spot the join. For Solomon here it was like that and it continued to be like that — one look (literally, one eye) was enough; even a small thing like a jewel in her necklace meant so much to him. It had stolen his heart. The word **'stolen'** is found only here. She takes his heart away; she captures it or, as Longman, following Keel, colloquially translates it, she drives him crazy. Literally she 'hearted' his heart. She ravished it. She made it beat faster.

This is a good thing for a husband or wife, or a potential husband and wife, to think about. What effect does my loved one have on me? Am I moved by his (or her) looks, actions and personality? Can you sing, 'Every little thing she does is magic'? We ought to be affected even by the small things in a way that is not true of anyone else. And if we look, we

shall find it to be so. We ought to encourage such thoughts in
ourselves.

Or to go yet higher, think about this phrase again. First
imagine how the beloved must have felt to hear King Solomon say such things. 'Why would he be interested in me?
How can what I do make such a difference?' Then think of
these words about the bride coming from Christ's lips! 'How
can it be?' we think. 'How can any little thing I do or say
make any difference to the King of the universe?' But such a
verse shows us that it does make a difference. You know,
believer, the Lord cannot take his eyes off you! He loves
you. The smallest things mean so much. I am sure we see
that sometimes, but too often we forget. We think that our
lives are insignificant, ordinary, dull and mundane. But they
are not when we know that he loves us. Even on the human
level, to know someone loves you makes such a difference:

Again I saw something meaningless under the sun:

There was a man all alone;
   he had neither son nor brother.
There was no end to his toil,
   yet his eyes were not content with his wealth.
'For whom am I toiling,' he asked,
   'and why am I depriving myself of enjoyment?'
This too is meaningless —
   a miserable business!
Two are better than one,
   because they have a good return for their work:
If one falls down,
   his friend can help him up.
But pity the man who falls
   and has no one to help him up!
Also, if two lie down together, they will keep warm.
   But how can one keep warm alone?

Though one may be overpowered,
two can defend themselves.
A cord of three strands is not quickly broken
(Eccles. 4:7-12).

How much more are these things so when we know that it
is our Creator and our God who is enthralled by us and at our
side!

3. The groom delights in his bride

The bridegroom then says:

How delightful is your love, my sister, my bride!
How much more pleasing is your love than wine,
and the fragrance of your perfume than any
spice!
Your lips drop sweetness as the honeycomb, my
bride;
milk and honey are under your tongue.
The fragrance of your garments is like that of
Lebanon
(4:10-11).

This is in the same vein. He delights in her. He loves
everything about her. Back at the beginning, she had said to
him, 'Your love is more delightful than wine' (1:2), and now
he returns the compliment. For him, the joy she gives is
better than wine. Her fragrant perfume is superior to any
spice. When she speaks, or perhaps better, when they kiss, it
is as sweet to him as wild honey on his tongue — milk and
honey flow. The description echoes Proverbs 5:3, but without the bitter pay-off that follows there. Her clothes also are
fragrant with the delights of Lebanon. She wears sweetly
perfumed and sensuous clothing.

This is how a man should think of his wife. This is how Christ speaks of the church. How unworthy we are! So often we are not delightful. Our lives lack fragrance. They are unsavoury. We are not a source of joy. Our lips drop bitterness. Poison and venom are under our tongues. We are crooked and harsh. How can Christ speak like this? He does so because all our sins are covered by his blood, which he has now poured out on the cross. He will make us perfect.

4. The groom thinks of his bride

> **You are a garden locked up, my sister, my bride;**
> **you are a spring enclosed, a sealed fountain.**
> **Your plants are an orchard of pomegranates**
> **with choice fruits,**
> **with henna and nard,**
> **nard and saffron,**
> **calamus and cinnamon,**
> **with every kind of incense tree,**
> **with myrrh and aloes**
> **and all the finest spices.**
> **You are a garden fountain,**
> **a well of flowing water**
> **streaming down from Lebanon**
>
> (4:12-15).

He uses two highly erotic images to describe the woman, or perhaps her intimate parts — a garden and a spring or fountain. The images are combined. Think of a water garden, or at least a garden with a stream or well in it. As with the honeyed lips, the image of the well has an antithetical parallel in Proverbs: 'A prostitute is a deep pit and a wayward wife is a narrow well' (Prov. 23:27). He finds her a garden **'locked up'** and an **'enclosed'**, or **'sealed'**, spring or fountain. In certain parts of central London there are gardens or small parks accessible only to local residents who are given a key to gain admittance. She is like one of those parks and he is the exclusive keyholder. For the first time he is about to enter.

She is a virgin on her wedding night, then. She has been inaccessible until now. The garden has been kept closed until this moment, the fountain sealed until this instant. The frozen waters have not been allowed to flow from Lebanon, not even for her own pleasure. The application to all unmarried people is clear. God has given you a lovely garden to look after. Keep it locked until the day of your marriage. The fountain is not to be unsealed until then, and then only for your spouse.

As believers we can think in similar terms of our spiritual chastity. We must keep ourselves pure until that day when Christ returns. See Proverbs 5:15-20, which, though construed in a slightly different way, covers the same ground and has reference to both the earthly and heavenly aspects of this.

Sibbes sees several analogies between gardens and the church. A garden is reclaimed from waste ground and cultivated with useful and delightful plants of various sorts. So believers are reclaimed from the world, having the weeds of sin removed and replaced by a range of things pleasing to God. A garden is a place for walking in and enjoying; it often has fountains and streams, and it needs constant attention. Christ and his Spirit are in the churches and always at work to improve them.

The man goes on to describe the plants in the garden or park (it is a rare Persian loanword from which we get our word 'paradise') — all sorts of mellow fruits and aromatic spices: pomegranates, choice fruits, henna, nard, saffron (a purple crocus), calamus (probably lemon grass or something similar), cinnamon, every kind of incense tree, myrrh, aloes (a fragrant wood from India), the finest spices. Whether these 'plants' are intended to signify various physical aspects of the woman is debatable. It is an exotic fantasy garden and there is no need to try to tie the individual elements to the various gifts that the Spirit gives. We know the different gifts he gives to believers. These must all be preserved and kept for Christ's enjoyment and use. They must not be perverted in any way.

The consummation of their love

1. How to respond to praise

Well, how does one respond to a paean of admiration like that? When it is genuine in this way and when it is given at the appropriate time, as this wedding night surely was, then the way to respond is the way that the bride does here:

> **Awake, north wind,**
> **and come, south wind!**
> **Blow on my garden,**
> **that its fragrance may spread abroad.**
> **Let my lover come into his garden**
> **and taste its choice fruits**
>
> (4:16).

So, taking up the image of the garden, she uses two further images in a beautiful description of the consummation. The first is that of wind blowing on the garden and so diffusing its beautiful aroma everywhere. The second depicts her lover as tasting the choicest fruits of her orchards.

The latter image is a fairly common one. People sometimes speak of adultery, for example, as eating forbidden fruit. The first image is much fresher, even though it may be similar in import to a clichéd, 'Be gentle with me'. Perhaps we lose something of its impact in the modern Western world by having so little experience of the aroma of an Eastern garden. I remember a Russian lady I knew who had lived in Persia talking to me about it and saying how poor an English garden is in contrast. Perhaps the problem is that we get so few warm breezes here as a rule. The image is particularly poignant for Christians when we remember how the Holy Spirit is so often spoken of as a wind (the word 'spirit' means wind). To adapt Sibbes, he is an invisible person who, like the wind, works on us to cleanse from sin, cool our tempers, search us out, stir us and refresh us, allowing nothing to stand in the way. This is how Christ comes to us in this life. We cannot be fragrant Christians without that work first taking place in us. With H. W. Baker let's pray:

> True Wind of Heav'n, from south or north,
> For joy or chastening, blow;
> The garden spices shall spring forth
> If thou wilt bid them flow.

Of course, the ultimate fulfilment is in the glory to come, at the consummation of all things. To this we look.

2. Love's consummation

In 5:1 we have the words of the bridegroom again:

> **I have come into my garden, my sister, my bride;**
> **I have gathered my myrrh with my spice.**
> **I have eaten my honeycomb and my honey;**
> **I have drunk my wine and my milk.**

He especially takes up the image of eating fruit and extends it to include gathering and drinking too. He enters that garden, locked until then but rightly and willingly opened up now, and he picks the flowers, as it were, and eats and drinks what is there — the sweet and nourishing honey and wine and milk. It is a very sensuous and evocative, even sexual, yet a pure and chaste description. We always ought to try to think of these matters in such terms. It is in this area that the world is, understandably, first and most effective in sullying and debasing. It is no easy task, but as Christians we ought to be active in reclaiming this area for Christ. He is sovereign over every part of life, including this one. The famous nineteenth-century Dutch theologian Abraham Kuyper once said that 'There is not a single inch in the whole domain of our human existence over which Christ, who is Sovereign over all, does not cry: "Mine!"' He was right and human existence includes this area as well as every other.

Solomon has in mind here both the delights of the marriage bed (the most fun you can have without laughing, according to Woody Allen) and, beyond that, the consummation to come in heaven between Christ and his bride, the church, and what leads up to it. If we feel uncomfortable noting the close parallels between the sexual act and mystical union with Christ, that is probably because of the degrading way in which the former is considered today. To divide these matters too sharply is a mistake.

Great efforts have been made, particularly in more recent years, with the rise of recreational sex, to separate marriage and the sex act. One writer speaks of the way some young people today 'have sexual intercourse with each other whenever they feel like it, the way they have a cup of coffee or a hamburger'. The idea is conceivable, of course, but it is clear from the Bible that this was never God's intention. As Italian actress Sophia Loren once observed, 'Sex without love is absolutely ridiculous.' Another actress, Shirley MacLaine, is one who has come to see that 'Sex is a serious undertaking.'

American Stanley Grenz, writing on sexual ethics, help-fully offers a threefold explanation of sex within the mar-riage bond. He says that:

1. It signifies the commitment of husband and wife to each other and recalls it. It is designed to represent and strengthen the marriage bond.
2. It is an act of mutual submission. It is a reciprocal expression of the desire to please one's spouse. Di-vorced from this setting, it almost inevitably becomes a selfish act.
3. Even when family planning is employed there is an open-endedness to the act; the idea of procreation is never entirely absent. Outside the marriage bed pro-creation is seldom desired.

Divorced from marriage, sex becomes a mere matter of pleasure-seeking and technique development — hence the sorts of unhelpful books and magazines that litter High Street newsagents and bookshops. Indulgence and performance are the new gods at whose feet we are urged to worship. They give a poor reward even for those able to master their dark secrets. The sexual act was intended for the marriage bed and once it is ripped from that context it slowly but surely becomes the meaningless monster, the hollow tormenter, that it is for so many today.

As for what sexual acts are permissible between a man and his wife, while being quite frank about certain acts outside the marriage bed, the Bible is noticeably silent on the matter. Married people are left to deal with such things for themselves and, provided they keep in mind all else that we read in Scripture about mutual respect, self-denial, the duty to make one's body available to one's partner, and similar matters, they should be able to come to a satisfactory answer regarding most questions that arise.

Spiritually, what glories lie ahead! As believers pray to
the winds to awaken and to their Lover to come into his
garden, so one day he will come in, and what a glorious
consummation that will be! Even now there are blessings,
too. Isaac Watts wrote a once well-known hymn based on
ideas in this passage:

> We are a garden walled around,
> Chosen and made peculiar ground;
> A little spot enclosed by grace
> Out of the world's wide wilderness.

> Like trees of myrrh and spice we stand,
> Planted by God the Father's hand;
> And all his springs in Zion flow,
> To make the young plantation grow.

> Awake, O heavenly wind, and come,
> Blow on this garden of perfume;
> Spirit divine! Descend and breathe
> A gracious gale on plants beneath.

> Make our best spices flow abroad,
> To entertain our Saviour God
> And faith, and love, and joy appear,
> And every grace be active here.

> Let my Beloved come and taste
> His pleasant fruits at his own feast:
> 'I come, my spouse, I come!' he cries,
> With love and pleasure in his eyes.

> Our Lord into his garden comes,
> Well pleased to smell our poor perfumes,

And calls us to a feast divine,
Sweeter than honey, milk, or wine.

'Eat of the tree of life, my friends,
The blessings that my Father sends;
Your taste shall all my dainties prove,
And drink abundance of my love.'

Jesus, we will frequent thy board,
And sing the bounties of our Lord;
But the rich food on which we live
Demands more praise than tongues can give.

Already our Lord is in his garden, as it were. Isn't this part of what the Lord's Supper symbolizes? There is more to come, however, when Christ returns. Are we looking forward to that day?

3. The encouragement given by others

Finally, hear the words of the friends again: **'Eat, O friends, and drink; drink your fill, O lovers'** (5:1). There is no jealousy here and no interference, only encouragement. That is how it should be for those of us who look on and see others falling in love and entering into the delights of marriage, whether we ourselves know those delights or not. As has already been mentioned, there is a Middle-Eastern tradition of wedding guests remaining around (elsewhere, of course) until the consummation. Perhaps that is why we have this chorus. This is not done in the West but the attitude is clearly to be commended. It reminds us again of the way the angels delight in everything to do with salvation (1 Peter 1:12). How they will rejoice with us who believe when Christ returns! Like the angels, we should even now be eager to look into everything to do with Christ and his kingdom.

To sum up

Husbands should love their wives as this man does. Our wives should seem more beautiful with each passing day. Christ, and his love for his people, is our model. As for our character as Christians, whoever we are, we ought to be gentle, innocent, lively, joyful, at peace and having a cheerful disposition, honest and sincere, being always upright yet tender. Christ is at work sanctifying us to this end. The work will be complete when he returns.

Virgins have a precious gift. They must take care how they handle it. We all ought to think often of the consummation of all things when Christ comes for his church. Then we shall know as we are now known; we shall see him as he is and be like him. The angels will gather the elect from every place, and all will be gathered in heaven, where there will be no more distress or fear.

If we are in love we ought to be affected by even little things that our loved one does. We may wonder how anything we do or say can affect the King of kings, but here we learn that it can. We are not ordinary or insignificant. The Lord cannot take his eyes off believers — he loves them so. We cannot be fragrant Christians without the work of the Spirit, however. What glories lie ahead! But even now we should pray for more of the Spirit and greater intimacy with Christ.

When you see others falling in love and enjoying the delights of marriage, you should be glad. As the angels delight in everything to do with salvation, so should we.

9.
Coldness: The loss of close covenant communion

Please read Song of Songs 5:2-8

As we examine the Song of Songs, what we are looking at and learning about is covenant love. We are learning, on one level, about human courtship and marriage, the covenant love between a man and his wife, and, on another, about God's covenant love towards his people and their response.

Already we have looked at the courting couple described in the opening chapters, the wedding procession and the wedding night. Next we turn to the beginning of the episode that starts in 5:2, and that is a more extreme form of the parallel crisis that threatened in 3:1-5. Once again we should be alert to its lessons on close covenant communion. We shall look first at what happens in 5:2-8, keeping the description given in 5:10-16, prompted by the question in 5:9, for the next chapter. All the words here are those of the Shulammite:

Shulammite	Friends	Solomon
5:2-8	—	—

She describes an imagined scene, the main details of which can probably be visualized with little difficulty.

It is night. Here is the woman of our story tucked up in bed. Though now married, she is alone. She is half asleep, half awake. Her husband is not there for some reason.

Then suddenly she hears him knocking at the door and calling out to her to open up for him and let him in. He is out in the cold and the damp night air. The quicker she can open up, the better. The obvious thing to do is to rush to the door and unlock it. But that is not what happens. Instead of going to the door she shouts out, 'I've gone to bed. I can't open the door for you. It's too much bother for me to get up.'

The man then starts to try to open the door some other way. She hears him and decides at last to go to him. However, by the time she reaches the door, he has gone. He has given up trying to get in and gone off somewhere else.

Now she is really unhappy. She starts calling after him and looking for him. She wanders away from the house and out into the streets of the city. The night watchmen spot her as she walks about and, thinking that she is up to no good, manhandle her and pull off the cloak that she had hastily thrown round her shoulders as she left the house. In desperation, she cries out to the women of Jerusalem to tell her where she can find her lover.

In some ways this is similar to the episode in chapter 3, only this time the dream seems more real, at least in certain parts. Throughout the sequence the spotlight alternates, switching from the woman to the man and then back again. It is a little like watching a tennis rally, or two people having an animated conversation — back and forth, back and forth, it goes. The scene reminds us of Shakespeare's words at the start of *A Midsummer Night's Dream.* Lysander says to Hermia, 'The course of true love never did run smooth.' This is true not only in courtship, but also even after a marriage has been consummated.

Some Christians become needlessly frustrated and disappointed because they do not have a perfect marriage. This can be especially acute if the courtship has been relatively brief and easy. You can imagine it. Here is a young Christian couple, Jack and Jessica. They met at a Christian conference, fell in love and were married within twelve months. It has been a blissful courtship, with hardly a cross word. Then they have their first major disagreement over something. They are shattered — not just because they have argued and perhaps said things that would have been better left unsaid, but because the illusion of a perfect marriage has now been well and truly blown. A passage like this shows us that even an idealized marriage like this one is likely to face problems. It is not good when that happens, of course, but it is important to see that this does not in any sense mean the end of the marriage.

Similarly, for those who have come to trust in Christ there can be unrealistic expectations about the Christian life. Here is a young man, Daniel. He has been converted a year and has read his Bible every day since. Then one busy day he is a little under the weather and, with one thing and another, he fails to find time to read Scripture and at the end of the day he falls asleep with his Bible open but unread. He wakes the next morning and realizes what has happened and is shattered by his failure.

Or take Becky. She gave her heart to the Lord six months ago and every day since she has found time to pray to the Lord, often with great fervour. However, this week has been a difficult one for her. Her mother is ill and there has been a change in her usual routine. One day she is so busy that she never really prays at all. You can imagine how she feels when she realizes. She feels deflated, discouraged, dismayed. Again this passage is here in part to remind us that there are no perfect Christians. We all fall short in many ways. It is how we cope with failure that matters.

Our all-too-common state

In 5:2 the beloved speaks. She says, **'I slept but my heart was awake.'** In other words, she was half asleep, half awake. It is clearly night-time, which in itself is a potent picture of the nature of the life we lead here on earth. The pictures of day and night, light and darkness, are used in different ways in Scripture. In one sense, becoming a Christian is seeing the light. It is passing from the ignorance and darkness of Satan's kingdom into the kingdom of light. However, in many ways it is still night-time while we are on earth — until Christ comes again and brings in a glorious new day. Because of this it is easy for us to grow sleepy and fail to watch. You remember how Jesus, when he wanted the disciples to pray with him in Gethsemane, sadly found them sleeping.

Alas, we have to say that most often Christians are found in a state of spiritual sleepiness. We are like the disciples in the Garden of Gethsemane. It may be that we are not sound asleep, but we are not fully awake either. So often in the history of the church that has been the general pattern. Our most common state is that of appearing to be asleep, although our hearts have been awakened and we are at least open to spiritual realities. Is that your state today? Is that often your condition? As we shall see, it is a dangerous situation to be in.

Sibbes considers what makes people sleepy. To avoid sleepiness, he says, shun the strong vapours of worldly care and desire; banish sorrow and weariness; beware of the music of flattery and deceit; eschew lack of spiritual exercise; beware of spiritual illness and keep away from lazy, yawning company.

There is also an application here to Christian marriages. Too often they are rather sleepy affairs. Things often muddle along fairly well, but there is a failure to be proactive and sometimes when a real strain does come, something gives way. Wives must take care not to grow cold towards husbands, and husbands must take care not to grow cold towards their wives. Fan the flames of fervent passion, stoke the fires of faithful commitment, or they will soon die down and go out.

A lover's plea

Next, she says:

> **Listen! My lover is knocking:**
> **Open to me, my sister, my darling,**
> **my dove, my flawless one.**
> **My head is drenched with dew,**
> **my hair with the dampness of the night**
>
> (5:2).

She can hear his knock at the door of the house that they share. He seeks and knocks and calls, and then waits. He wants her to open the door and for him to come in to her. Such language is sexually charged. A door opening for a man to come in could be a metaphor for sexual union. If we pursue this line too closely, however, we shall undoubtedly run into difficulties of interpretation.

He calls her by four different terms of affection, each preceded by the possessive pronoun, **'my'**: **'my sister'**, **'my dove'**, **'my darling'** and **'my flawless one'**. The word 'my' is thus repeated, emphasizing their unity. The terms themselves form something of a crescendo and focus, in turn, on their family nearness, his care for her, her purity and her perfect dignity.

We are talking about terms of endearment, what are often called 'pet names'. There are a host of alternatives — 'honey', 'sugar', 'sweetie', 'sweetheart'; 'dear', 'dearie', 'dearest', 'pet'; 'babe', 'baby'; 'beloved', 'gorgeous', 'love', 'lovely'; 'precious', 'treasure'; 'heart'. Some are overused and lose their power. 'Acushla' is a rather pleasing Irish one. It means 'my pulse'. 'My better half' has some charm perhaps; 'significant other' much less. Bob Dylan's term, 'covenant woman', appeals. A Christian husband may not use any of these expressions often, or at all (though perhaps he should); however, he should certainly think of his wife in such terms as we find here.

My sister

He has already used this term in 4:9 – 5:1. In the New Testament, married believers are considered joint-heirs of the kingdom. Therefore, husbands are to 'be considerate as you live with your wives, and treat them with respect as the weaker partner and as heirs with you of the gracious gift of life, so that nothing will hinder your prayers' (1 Peter 3:7).

The Christian wife is not some sort of inferior, second-rate person who gets her religion via her husband. No, they are joint-heirs; both are priests to God. Her calling as a wife is to submit to her husband in the marriage bond, but they nevertheless stand before God as equals — saved sinners both, brother and sister in the Lord, by the grace of God. If you have a Christian wife she is not only your wife but also your sister in the Lord. One day in heaven, though no longer your wife, she will still be your sister.

My darling

Love must be there for any marriage to work, of course. It is the calling of the husband, above all, to love his wife. Whether he calls her 'darling' or not, he must show his wife that he loves her. Isaac sets a pattern for us here. We read of Rebecca that 'She became his wife, and he loved her.' He also showed that love to her by caressing her (Gen. 24:67;

26:8). The New Testament is clear on this: 'Husbands, love your wives, just as Christ loved the church and gave himself up for her' (Eph. 5:25).

My dove

In the New Testament husbands are also told not to be stern with their wives: 'Husbands, love your wives and do not be harsh with them' (Col. 3:19). They must always be gentle. They should never shout. They should never be brusque or callous. Cruelty and insensitivity are out. Think of your wife as a pure, gentle white dove and treat her accordingly.

My flawless one

Husbands must respect their wives. They must treat them with the utmost dignity and honour. When we speak to them or about them, that is paramount. Names such as, 'her indoors', 'she who must be obeyed', 'the boss', 'ball and chain', 'trouble and strife' and even 'my old lady', 'the wife' or 'the missus', should be avoided unless used with the utmost good nature (Luther was able to get away with 'my lord, Katie' and 'my chain'!). In a society where some young men are growing up to think that 'bitch', 'cow', or even more offensive terms, are perfectly acceptable ways of referring to women, a wind is being sown that when reaped will prove a whirlwind.

Now the great model for all this is the Lord Jesus Christ. This is how he speaks of his people. He is our elder brother. He is full of love for his own. How gently he treats us, and how pure he desires us to be! He justifies us from every sin by his death on the cross so that when he sees us, he views us as flawless.

Here we have pictured this perfect loving one seeking, knocking, calling and waiting. Inevitably Christians think of the words of Jesus: 'Here I am! I stand at the door and knock. If anyone hears my voice and opens the door, I will come in and eat with him, and he with me' (Rev. 3:20). That verse has often been used evangelistically but, like this one in the Song, it speaks primarily to sleepy Christians who are neglecting close covenant communion with the Saviour. Here in the Song of Solomon it is the same Saviour, the loving Bridegroom, who stands at the door and knocks but is not given admittance.

How does Christ knock at our doors? Sibbes speaks of his mercies, corrections, the preaching of the Word, the example of others, the Spirit's labours and the varied work of conscience. All these are knocks at the doors of our hearts.

His wait is detrimental. He has no place to lay his head and his **'head is drenched with dew'**, his hair **'with the dampness of the night'**. However we apply that, it is true that we are often thoughtless, unfeeling and callous towards our Saviour. We make him an outsider. He becomes afresh the unwanted Christ of Bethlehem, the despised Christ of Nazareth, the lonely Christ of Gethsemane and the rejected Christ of Golgotha. In 1867 W. W. How wrote:

Shame on us, Christian brothers,
His name and sign who bear,
Oh shame, thrice shame upon us,
To keep him standing there! ...

Oh love that passeth knowledge,
So patiently to wait!
Oh sin that hath no equal,
So fast to bar the gate!

Our all-too-common response

So how does this woman respond to this wonderfully loving approach? Who could fail to respond positively? Yet in 5:3 we read that she says:

> **I have taken off my robe —**
> **must I put it on again?**
> **I have washed my feet —**
> **must I soil them again?**

Like the foolish virgins in Jesus' parable, she is not ready. There could be a reference here to the fact that she does not want to make the effort that a sexual union would involve. 'I have a headache,' would be the modern euphemism. More probably she is saying, 'I'm in bed now, I'm all cosy and snug. I'm not getting up and getting dressed again to come to you. I'm not walking across the dirty floor to open up for you.' Now she is half asleep, of course, and we can forgive a lot when people are not fully alert, but it does show a fearful disregard for this ardent and devoted lover. Instinctively we feel that she is in the wrong. Why did she not wait up for him? She must have known that he was coming. He may have been delayed, of course. At the very least she could have arranged something with the key. Her attitude is clearly wrong. It shows a distinct lack of love and care.

This is a danger in any marriage. Things will only work if there is give and take. Selfishness destroys the bliss of married life. Self-interest undercuts every effort at love and harmony. If we think only of ourselves — our needs, our comfort — then things cannot work. It is no good when one side is wooing and pursuing while the other is balking at it and rejecting it.

On the specific matter of conjugal rights or sexual union Paul is clear: 'The husband should fulfil his marital duty to his wife, and likewise the wife to her husband. The wife's body does not belong to her alone but also to her husband. In the same way, the husband's body does not belong to him alone but also to his wife. Do not deprive each other except by mutual consent and for a time, so that you may devote yourselves to prayer. Then come together again so that Satan will not tempt you because of your lack of self-control' (1 Cor. 7:3-5).

These verses in the Song typify our attitude to Christ too often, as well. They remind us of the phrase from Jesus' parable of the great banquet: 'But they all alike began to make excuses' (Luke 14:18). The Lord comes near with winning words and wooing actions, but we do not want to know. How many times have we woken in the morning thinking we ought to begin with the Scriptures but have been somehow reluctant? How slow we are to pray! How unwilling we sometimes are to sit under the preaching of the Word! We make ourselves so comfortable in this world that at times we are unwilling to make the effort necessary to draw near to him. Our way is blocked by non-existent snags; we refuse to deny ourselves; the kingdom takes second place; we forget that drawing near to Christ is in our own best interests; we forget our calling; we are preoccupied and dreamy. There is still too much worldliness, corruption and hypocrisy in us, too great a willingness to justify ourselves and to make the laziness of others an excuse for our own sloth.

Is that you at the present time? Christ is wooing you today. 'Here I am! I stand at the door and knock,' he says. 'If anyone hears my voice and opens the door, I will come in and eat with him, and he with me.' 'Open to me, my sister', is his cry, 'my darling, my dove, my flawless one.' But you cannot be bothered to make the effort. You are reading this book. That is good. But you are not willing to go any further or to make any more effort. That is bad. Best put the book down and cry out for him to draw near and bless. Go to God, not to men. Pray for heavenly wisdom, for resolution, for strong conviction, for willingness to suffer and for a realistic view of our situation. Pray to be God-centred, sin-hating, grace-loving and fully set on the glory to come. Labour for faith to believe the truth and for your heart to be warmed with love for Christ. Enough time has been wasted. There is no guarantee that we shall have another such opportunity on earth to seek him.

A lover's insistence

Where they were used, keys in those far-off days tended to be much larger than those we use today. Often there was room enough for a hand to fit into the keyhole. Often there was no key, just a latch. Here she says, **'My lover thrust his hand through the latch-opening'** (5:4). She looks towards the door, where she sees that he is trying to let himself in by putting his hand through the opening in an effort to unhitch the latch.

Sometimes in the marriage relationship it can be like that. One or other is trying to get into the other's life, as it were; trying to find a way of reconnecting, of relating again one to the other. It is frustrating. If the other person would simply open the door a little, entry would be easy, but they simply refuse. He or she remains all shut up to you.

When this happens we must try to find a way in wherever we can. Sometimes there is a shared interest, although many husbands and wives differ in their tastes and hobbies. Where both husband and wife are Christians there is always the gospel that unites, although there is room for disagreement on certain things even there. A marriage is only going to work if, when there are barriers between the two, when there is a door in the way, both work at opening it (and not with each tugging in opposite directions!).

Something similar can be said about the relationship between Christ and his people. The Pre-Raphaelite artist William Holman Hunt painted a famous picture of Jesus standing at the door and knocking. Called *The Light of the World*, the main version can be seen in St Paul's Cathedral in London. It is often noted that the latch of the door is on the inside. That is correct. Christ is sovereign and he is the one who opens the door of the heart in conversion. However, when he speaks to the believer, he calls on him to open the door. As here, he will sometimes thrust his hand through the latch-hole insistently, but we notice in this passage that that is not enough to gain him entry. Christ is insistent. He wants to come into your life. However, it is up to you, believer, to act upon his invitations.

The proper response

So, having now been fully woken up, the woman begins to react as she should have done from the beginning. Note the four stages.

Firstly, **'My heart began to pound for him'** (5:4). Her heart was awake at the beginning of all this but now it is pounding. It is racing. She can hear it and feel it. Oh, how she wants to see her lover! Oh, how she wants to hold him! We must come to that stage as Christians. Too often we are slow and sluggish, dawdling and drowsy. Our hearts are not beating very fast, sometimes hardly at all. We need to stir ourselves up on occasions. This is the point of preaching — to stir us up by setting before us Christ and what he has done.

Secondly, **'I arose to open for my lover'** (5:5). Then, at last, she does something about it. Durham says that 'Repentance when real will put the most careless on their feet.' Again that is what we need to do. Do you want to pray? Then get out of bed and pray. Put this book down and get on your knees. Do you want to read his Word? Then get up and read. Put this book to one side for a while and get out your unread Bible.

Thirdly, '**... my hands dripped with myrrh, my fingers with flowing myrrh, on the handles of the lock**' (5:5). Next, she takes hold of the lock to open the door. There is myrrh everywhere. Where has it come from? Maybe from him — he had put his hand through the hole of the lock. Sibbes suggests it comes from him and signifies God's grace to us even in times of desertion. Maybe it comes from her — perhaps she had dipped her hands in it as she went towards the door. If so, it was meant as a sign of welcome to him. She is certainly in a very different mood from that which she had showed at first, when he had been knocking. Now she wants to do everything she can to open up and to welcome him in. That is how we should be at the first sign of Jesus' coming near.

Fourthly, '**I opened for my lover**' (5:6). Here is where the pounding heart, the getting up and the fiddling with the lock have all been leading. She wants to get that door open and to see her lover. If only she had reacted like this sooner! This is how we should be in our relationships with our husbands or wives — more than ready to open up to them; alert and responsive to their very first approaches; eager to remove any barrier that stands between, whatever it may be. This is how we ought to be as regards close covenant communion with Christ too. Nothing must hinder our fellowship with him.

A lover's departure

And then comes the tragic anticlimax: '**... but my lover had left; he was gone**' (6:6). How often that is the experience on both the human level and the spiritual one! A wife has waited and waited for her wild man to calm down, for her neglectful husband to pay her attention, for her roving spouse to settle — but it has never happened. Then a day has come when the man finally decides he really wants his wife's company. But he cannot have it. She may not have actually left him, but her time is taken up elsewhere, her openness to him is not what it was, and he misses out. A husband has longed and longed for his headstrong wife to give in, for his uninterested wife to pay him some attention, for his wayward spouse to settle — but it has never happened. Then a day has come when the woman suddenly decides she really wants her husband's company. But she cannot have it. He may still be around, but his time is spent on other things, his openness to her is not what it was, and she misses out. Time and tide wait for no man and if we take our spouses for granted and presume that they will always be willing to fit in with us, we may have a rude awakening one day.

On the spiritual plane, we must reckon with the possibility of either losing access to a means of grace that we have enjoyed, or of a sense of inward spiritual desertion. A good preacher may be removed; a faithful church may close. You may be cut off from fellowship by illness or some other circumstance. A mistake that we often make is to suppose that because God is eternal, patient, unchanging and can always be sought, we can leave such times to our own convenience. For example, we think of how 'when I am older', 'when the kids are off my hands', or 'later today' or 'at another time' we will be more prayerful and seek God. However, reality is not like that. The fact is that for various reasons there are seasons when God draws near. If we do not take full advantage of such seasons then and there, we shall probably not have the opportunity again. We can see this, I trust, on the human level. Children grow up all too quickly. The right circumstances at home often do not materialize.

There is a mystery here but we must recognize it. The nineteenth-century Scots minister and theology professor Rabbi Duncan once started to pray before a lecture and then

proceeded to pray throughout the lecture period. This understandably annoyed some of the students, who were concerned
to learn and to pass their examinations. Professor Duncan
explained that, 'having gotten in', he was loath to leave off.
The man was an eccentric, of course, but he had a point.

The inevitable response

Then we read of what the woman did when she realized that
her lover had gone. She says, **'My heart sank at his depart-
ure'**, or possibly, 'My heart longed for his speaking' (5:6).
On the basis of the NIV translation we can say that she was
devastated. This is what one would expect. This is how a
person would be if their husband or wife left them, or even
just went off and they did not know where. If we deliberately
push people away, the boot may soon be on the other foot.

There can be nothing worse for the believer than a sense
of spiritual desertion. Here in Britain we are experiencing it
as a nation at the present time — it can come to churches and
to individuals too. At such times God's people long for his
voice to be heard.

This new crisis takes the woman out of the warmth,
intimacy and privacy of the bedroom into the cold, forbid-
ding and public streets. **'I looked for him but did not find
him,'** she says. **'I called him but he did not answer.'** How
frustrating! Do you know anything about this? Why does it
happen? Sometimes it is an enigma. At other times we can
trace it back to our own sinful neglect. Seek to avoid such
things. If you are in that situation, persevere. Who knows
when a season of refreshing may come again?

> **The watchmen found me**
>   **as they made their rounds in the city.**
> **They beat me, they bruised me;**

they took away my cloak,
those watchmen of the walls!

(5:7).

It is difficult to be sure how to take these words. This woman tells us that she underwent pain and humiliation at the hands of those who were really supposed to be there to protect her from such things. It was a case, no doubt, of mistaken identity. Such suffering at the hands of friends can be the lot of those who search for Christ but do not find him. When ministers do their duty and simply preach the Word faithfully, they can inadvertently terrify and hurt God's children if these children are undergoing spiritual desertion as the preachers tear away at them and expose their sins. 'They turn persecutors,' says Owen. The minister will speak of the importance of assurance, of knowing God's presence and make similar statements. He is describing the normal Christian life. For those who are suffering spiritual desertion this can only add to their sorrow and sadness.

O daughters of Jerusalem, I charge you —
**   if you find my lover,**
what will you tell him?
**   Tell him I am faint with love.**

Finally, we note her plea in 5:8. We have already had the phrase: 'Daughters of Jerusalem, I charge you', in longer form, in 2:7 and 3:5. In 2:5 she has spoken of being 'faint with love', but here there is a different shade of meaning as her lover has now gone. Are you like this at present? Are you faint with love? Are you desperate to find the Saviour again? Then good Christian people will pray for you, if you ask them. They will tell the Saviour all about it. Just let them know your case.

To sum up

The best marriages face problems. Wisdom recognizes this.
Too often Christian marriages merely tick over. Real strains
come and something snaps. Husbands and wives must not
grow cold towards each other. Tend the fires of passion.
Christian husbands must see their wives as equals. You are
joint-heirs, brothers in Christ, priests to God. Wives must
submit to husbands, but as sinners saved by grace they are on
a par. Husbands, love your wives. Always respect them. Do
not be harsh. Take care what terms you use when speaking
to, or about, them.

Marriage only works where there is give and take. Selfishness destroys. When one side seeks and the other spurns,
failure follows. Teamwork is vital. If communication fails, a
way back must be found. If you take others for granted and
refuse to liaise, a day may well come when you want support
and there will be none.

It is important not to be unrealistic about the Christian
life. We are bound to fail at certain points. How we cope
with failure is crucial. Too often we are not as we should be.
We are often caught napping — a dangerous condition.
Christ stands at the door knocking. He gently speaks words
of love, but we spurn him. We make no effort to go to him.
He is insistent, but it is up to us to act on his invitations. Why
are we not more eager? We need to stir ourselves. This is the
purpose of preaching. We must respond. Nothing must be
allowed to hinder fellowship.

Part of the problem is supposing that we can go to God
when we wish. In truth there are seasons when God draws
near. If we fail to take advantage of them, they will be gone.
If this is a barren time for you, persist in seeking the Lord.
Who knows when seasons of refreshing may return? Are you
faint with love? Are you desperate to find the Saviour again?
Do not be dispirited, but ask other Christians to pray for you.

10.
Captivation: True beauty and where it is found

Please read Song of Songs 5:9 – 6:12

Joni Mitchell's sixties protest song, 'Big yellow taxi', is her most famous. Along with all the complaints about DDT and toxic waste, the refrain includes the phrase:

> Don't it always go to show
> You don't know what you got 'til it's gone?

There is nothing about urbanization, pollution or deforestation in the Song of Songs, but these lines may provide a sort of secular text for this particular section.

In 5:2-8 we have a description of the groom coming home late and finding the door locked and his bride in bed. She is reluctant to open the door, even though he calls and knocks with some persistence. By the time that she eventually comes to the door he is no longer there, having given up trying to get in and gone elsewhere. In her unhappiness she starts calling after him and looks for him everywhere. She wanders into the city, where the nightwatchmen spot her and, thinking she is up to no good, manhandle her and pull off the cloak that she threw round her shoulders as she hurried out. In desperation she cries out to the women of Jerusalem to tell her where she can find her lover.

Such a passage has a great deal to teach us about how often as believers our fellowship with the Lord is not what it should be. Too often we are deaf to his calls and his pleadings. Then when we suddenly decide that we do want fellowship with him after all, it does not happen, and so we are in despair.

We now want to look at the subject as it unfolds in 5:9 – 6:12. First, we have a description of her lover by the beloved, then something about what had gone wrong in their relationship. Next, there is another description of the beloved and something more about what had happened. Finally, there is a call to return. As we are continually seeing, this love story can be understood on both horizontal and vertical levels. Here we are again thinking particularly of how it applies vertically — the relationship between Christ and his church.

The pattern of dialogue is probably as follows:

Shulammite	Friends	Solomon
—	5:9	—
5:10-16	—	—
—	6:1	—
6:2-3	—	—
—	—	6:4-9
—	6:10	—
—	—	6:11-12

The beauty of the bridegroom

In response to her plea for help in finding her lover, the daughters of Jerusalem ask the Shulammite:

How is your beloved better than others,
   most beautiful of women?
How is your beloved better than others,
   that you charge us so?

(5:9).

In other words, 'What makes your lover so special, then?'
This leads to another *wasf*. The previous one, at the beginning of chapter 4, was his description of her given in her
presence. This is her description of him in his absence. It is
again symbolic language, no doubt. It reminds us a little of
the description of the glorified Lord Jesus given by John in
Revelation 1. Having lost sight of her lover, the beloved
remembers just how wonderful he is. In longing to see him
again, she is taken up with a description of his glory.

What she says here can be applied chiefly to the Lord
Jesus Christ. All true Christians can give a description of the
Saviour they love. We ought to be constantly reminding
ourselves of his beauty and wonder. Let us consider some
aspects highlighted by this passage.

1. He is outstanding

She begins by saying, **'My lover is radiant and ruddy,
outstanding among ten thousand'** (5:10). He shines out. In
human terms, he is a picture of health. There is a glow about
him. He is ruddy, like David in his youth (1 Sam 16:12;
17:42). He is like a standard-bearer at the head of a large
army — prominent, a leader of men. She could spot him with
ease. Even from among ten thousand she could pick him out
without difficulty. 'One in a million' may be an equivalent
phrase today. He is exceptional. No one compares with him.
This, of course, is the truth about Christ. Though 'his appearance was so disfigured beyond that of any man and his

form marred beyond human likeness' (Isa. 52:14), no one
can begin to compare with him. He is the Holy One of God.
There follows a head-to-toe description.

2. *His noble character*

She begins with his head:

> **His head is purest gold;**
> **his hair is wavy**
> **and black as a raven**
>
> (5:11).

He is not simply a king with a crown. His very head is gold.
There is something divine about him, something glorious and
lasting. His hair is not grey with age, but black as a raven's
and full of body. Christ is eternally youthful and his thoughts
are many and deep. In Christ 'are hidden all the treasures of
wisdom and knowledge' (Col. 2:3). How noble her lover is,
and how noble is Christ, the King of kings! Sibbes urges us,
therefore, to keep him as head and no other, to labour to live
in a way that suits such a head and to cast all our crowns at
his feet (Rev. 4:10).

3. *His tenderness*

She then says:

> **His eyes are like doves**
> **by the water streams,**
> **washed in milk,**
> **mounted like jewels**
>
> (5:12).

In the light of the poetical structure some want to add a reference to teeth here: 'His eyes are like doves by the water streams. *His teeth* are washed in milk, mounted like jewels.' That could work, but it is conjecture and, with Longman, we shall therefore reject the emendation.

We have noted before how commonly doves are mentioned in this book and the various ways in which such references can be understood. **'Doves ... washed in milk'** would appear to be a mixed metaphor — something that is taboo in English, but fine in Hebrew. Perhaps the idea is of doves washing themselves whiter in milk. Alternatively, there is such a thing as dove's milk, secreted by adult birds feeding their young. The picture of a chick's mouth wide open while dove's milk swills around it could suggest an eye, but this is something of a conjecture. No doubt the white of the eyes is in mind, however, and the word **'streams'** probably refers to the glistening tears of love in his eyes. His pupils are perfectly set, as jewels might be — not too close together or too far apart, not too deep set or protruding. All this conveys a picture both of discernment and of great tenderness and compassion in judgement. Jesus looks with kindness upon sinners like us. He looks with love and tenderness, compassion and pity. Full of understanding and concern, how kind and sympathetic he is! How he weeps when we sin!

4. His richness and profusion

In 5:13 she begins: **'His cheeks are like beds of spice yielding perfume.'** It may well be that she is thinking of her lover's beard. A full beard was the norm for men throughout Israel's history. Female attitudes to beards vary. It is often a matter of weighing up look against feel! By way of digression I quote C. C. Bombaugh:

With whiskers thick upon my face I went my fair to
    see;
She told me she could never love a bear-faced chap
    like me.
I shaved them clean and called again, and thought my
    troubles o'er;
She laughed outright, and said I was more bare-faced
    than before.

If it is the beard that is in mind, perhaps it was literally
perfumed, by accident or design. Manliness and courage are
emphasized. Looking higher, Isaiah describes how the
Lord's beard was plucked from his cheeks. By his suffering
and death he, as it were, released fragrant perfume, the
perfume of his saving work. Everything about him is characterized by richness, fulness, abundance.

5. His fragrant words

She continues: **'His lips are like lilies dripping with
myrrh'** (5:13) — another reference to lilies and to perfume,
to myrrh in particular. Her lips drip honey (4:11); his lips
drip myrrh. The lilies are presumably red flowers of some
description, not what we think of as lilies today. Again, there
is a sense of fulness, of abundance, and a reference to
Christ's humanity. We remember that when he spoke, people
were amazed. They had never heard anyone speak as he
spoke. He still speaks today in his Word, and what a world
there is in it! What wonderful things come from it! There
'endless glories shine'. Every line drips fragrance. Hear his
Word and obey it. Those who do so are blessed.

6. *His gracious works*

'His arms are rods of gold set with chrysolite' (5:14). It is not entirely clear what jewel is in mind here. It is called *'Tarshish'*. Perhaps it is a beryl or topaz, possibly olivine, onyx or black jet. The picture could be of literal bracelets on his arms, but is more likely to be of arms or hands made up of golden rings or rods — suggesting perhaps ripples of muscle — and then probably it is the fingers that are set with yellow jewels. It speaks of the lover's strength and his ability to protect and help his beloved. It includes the idea of hands full of blessing. Certainly the Lord Jesus is active for his people. He works for those who trust in him. He provides for them and upholds them at all times.

7. *His strength*

'His body is like polished ivory decorated with sapphires' (5:14). We are thinking here of symmetry and, once more, of the beauty of his lithe body, which conveys the idea of strength. The word for **'body'** could be translated 'bowels'. In that case his compassion is probably in mind. Commentators who see a more intimate reference here forget that the beloved is speaking to the daughters of Jerusalem. We shall take this phrase with the first part of 5:15: **'His legs are pillars of marble set on bases of pure gold.'** Marble speaks of smoothness and strength. Gold speaks of imperishability, of unshakeable foundations. Here, and in the rest of the verse, we find allusions to materials used in the temple, and that is perhaps not without significance.

Taking these images together, we are presented with the picture of one who is solid and strong. He is immovable, invincible, unassailable. No one can stand against him. The victory is always his and if we are under his protection we need fear nothing.

8. His splendid appearance

She continues: **'His appearance is like Lebanon, choice as its cedars'** (5:15). We are speaking here of his overall appearance, his bearing or stance. There is something striking and commanding about the very look of him. Even the way he stands is wonderful to behold. His bearing demands respect. How stately his manner! It is like looking at a forest of tall, strong cedars of Lebanon. As one writer puts it, cut down one tree; thousands remain: 'Nothing will ever diminish the infinite and eternal Son of God.'

9. His sweetness

Next we read, **'His mouth is sweetness itself'** (5:16). The word translated **'his mouth'** is more literally 'his palate'. Not just in his words (which we know are sweeter than the honeycomb), but in his sweet kisses of affection and in the very way he looks, we see sweetness personified. How kind, how loving, how pleasant, how tender, how welcoming, he is!

10. His loveliness

It is summed up in the final phrase: **'He is altogether lovely.'** No one can match him. He is most desirable, most attractive. He is incomparable, unrivalled, unsurpassed. Without equal, he reigns supreme. In applying this verse to Christ John Owen uses the word 'lovely' eleven times over. He speaks of how lovely Christ is with regard to his person, birth, life, death, resurrection and ascension, glory and majesty, grace and consolations, tender care, power and wisdom, ordinances, vengeance and pardon. 'What shall I say?' he concludes. 'He is altogether lovely.'

Sibbes asks how Christ was lovely when he was flogged and wore the crown of thorns and was crucified between thieves. By way of answer he refers to the story of King Alphonsus, who one day saw a poor man pulling his animal out of a ditch and went to help him. After this act of condescension, says Sibbes, 'his subjects ever loved him the better'.

Other writers draw attention to Christ's twofold nature (that he is both God and man), his threefold offices of Prophet, Priest and King, his many titles (there are over 150) and the many ways in which he is presented in Scripture. He is the woman's seed crushing Satan, the Passover Lamb, the High Priest entering heaven for his people, the pillar of cloud and fire, the Prophet greater than Moses, the captain of our salvation, the Judge, the Kinsman-Redeemer, the Anointed One, the perfect King, the faithful scribe, the one who rebuilds broken walls, the Saviour, the Defender, the Lord and Shepherd, the Lover and Bridegroom (as we see in this very book).

He is also Everlasting Father, Prince of peace, Wonderful Counsellor, Mighty God, the righteous Branch, the weeping Prophet, the wheel that turns in all directions, the Son of Man who is with us in the fire, the longsuffering Husband, the one who pours out the Spirit, the one who bears our burdens, the great resurrected missionary, the messenger with beautiful feet, the avenger of God's elect, the great evangelist who cries for revival, the restorer of God's lost heritage, the cleansing fountain, the King who brings peace and humbly rides on a colt, and the Sun of Righteousness risen with healing in his wings!

Further, he is the Messiah, the wonder-working Servant, the perfect man, the Son of God, the ascended Lord, the one who justifies sinners, our wisdom, righteousness, sanctification and redemption, one who sets men free, our riches, our peace, our God who meets every need, the fulness of the

Godhead, the soon-coming King, the one mediator between God and man, the faithful pastor, the Friend who sticks closer than a brother, the one greater than all whose blood washes away sin, the Great Shepherd and Bishop of our souls, everlasting love, the keeper of our souls, the Lamb slain and the Lion of Judah, the King of kings and Lord of lords!

No wonder Augustus Toplady could write:

Compared with Christ, in all beside
No comeliness I see;
The one thing needful, dearest Lord,
Is to be one with thee.

Do we feel the same? Can we agree with Toplady's contemporary John Berridge, the vicar of Everton? He wrote in the same vein as these verses in the Song:

If gazing strangers want to know
What makes me sing of Jesus so;
I love his name, 'tis very dear,
And would his loveliness declare:
A single smile from Jesus given
Will lift a drooping soul to heaven.

His eyes are full of melting love,
More soft and sparkling than the dove;
And sweet instruction he conveys,
To warm my heart and guide my ways:
A single smile from Jesus given
Will lift a drooping soul to heaven...

His mercies, like himself, endure,
And like his love are ever sure;
And when our eyes his worth can view,

Our hearts will love and trust him too,
A single smile from Jesus given
Will lift a drooping soul to heaven.

Sibbes has four 'uses' or applications for this text. He says, 'Let us then rest upon his obedience and righteousness'; 'Let us labour to be in him'; 'Here only we have whereupon to spend the marrow of our best affections.' His final 'use' asks four questions to test whether Christ is altogether lovely to us. How do you value Christ? Are you ready to suffer for him? Does it show in the way you speak? Do you know that holy discontent which is an inevitable part of life on earth? Finally, he calls on us to 'labour to make our sins bitter and loathsome, that Christ may be sweet'; 'to attend upon the means of salvation, to hear the unsearchable riches of Christ' and to 'join with company that highly esteem of Christ, and such as are better than ourselves'.

Although our main application here is to Jesus Christ, there is a lesson on the horizontal level too. For husbands, or prospective husbands, here is the perfect model. This is how we should seek to be. It is rather embarrassing for most of us if we take it on the purely physical level. What an even greater challenge, however, if we see beyond that to the spiritual meaning! Are we noble, tender, fragrant, gracious, strong and sweet? Are our looks, words and actions towards our wives what they should be? What a challenge, indeed! As for wives, maybe they can learn here about loving their husbands, or being affectionate to them, something that Paul tells Titus older women must teach younger ones to do (Titus 2:4).

The beloved concludes: **'This is my lover, this my friend, O daughters of Jerusalem'** (5:16). Is Christ your Lover? Is he your Friend? We have every reason to be proud of him. We have every reason to be confident in him. He is ideal. Give thanks for such a perfect Saviour. If you do not

know him, I urge you to consider this portrait, then come to
him and put your faith in him today. Do not delay. To quote
Watts once again:

> All over glorious is my Lord,
> Must be beloved, and yet adored;
> His worth if all the nations knew,
> Sure the whole earth would love him too.

Where the bridegroom is to be found

As we come into chapter 6, we remind ourselves that this
wonderful description was prompted by a sense of deso-
lation. This magnificent lover is apparently lost. He is
nowhere to be found. What poignancy that adds to the
description! The beloved is full of desire for him, but does
not know where he is. The women of Jerusalem are now
convinced that this woman is seeking a paragon of beauty in
her lover, so they say to her:

> **Where has your lover gone,**
>   **most beautiful of women?**
> **Which way did your lover turn,**
>   **that we may look for him with you?**
>
> (6:1).

They are eager to help her, but it is not they who, in fact,
find him. It is not they who give the answer as to where he is,
but the beloved herself. Now, of course, this is something of
a dream sequence, a mystical and poetic reverie, full of
symbolism, and so it comes out in a slightly strange way.
There is a great lesson for us here, nevertheless. We can
arrive at it by answering three straightforward questions:

1. Where is he to be found?

She says, **'My lover has gone down to his garden, to the beds of spices...'** (6:2). Where is that? Well, we have already learned that **'his garden'** is a reference to the beloved herself, and especially to the place where they meet. If the phrase **'gone down'** is important it is in underlining the idea of condescension. Where is Jesus to be found? He is in his church, with his people. Yes, but the whole problem was that he was not there. He was there, of course, when he had come for her, but she had brushed him off and he had gone. Then what happened? She went to look for him. Yes, and at first she did not find him. But then, it appears, as she described him, she remembered how wonderful he was and they were reunited. It sounds bizarre in real terms but believers know the experience in practice. We are backslidden or cold; we are estranged from the Lord. Then we come into his presence in church, or we start reading about him at home, or someone speaks to us about him, or we start speaking about him ourselves for some reason, and our hearts are strangely warmed. We begin to remember his glory and beauty and wonder; then, suddenly, somehow, he is there with us once again.

2. Why did he come to his garden?

He came to the garden **'to browse in the gardens and to gather lilies'** (6:2). This idea of browsing has already come up in 2:16 and 4:5. It expresses intimacy. Christ loves nothing better than to enjoy the delight of his people's intimate presence. He gathers lilies there, as it were, lilies of praise. It astounds us to think of it, but we must never forget the great delight that God has in his people. How he loves to graze there! How he loves to gather flowers from among us! 'The LORD delights in those who fear him, who put their hope in his unfailing love' (Ps. 147:11). 'For the LORD takes delight in his people; he crowns the humble with salvation' (Ps. 149:4).

There are prophecies to this end too:

No longer will they call you Deserted,
    or name your land Desolate.
But you will be called Hephzibah [my delight is in
    her],
    and your land Beulah [married];
for the LORD will take delight in you,
    and your land will be married.
As a young man marries a maiden,
    so will your sons marry you;
as a bridegroom rejoices over his bride,
    so will your God rejoice over you

(Isa. 62:4-5).

I will rejoice over Jerusalem
    and take delight in my people;
the sound of weeping and of crying
    will be heard in it no more

(Isa. 65:19).

The LORD your God is with you,
    he is mighty to save.
He will take great delight in you,
    he will quiet you with his love,
    he will rejoice over you with singing

(Zeph. 3:17).

Think of Jesus finding the missing lamb and how he 'joyfully puts it on his shoulders and goes home', calling on all to rejoice with him.

3. What is the bride's response?

The bride says, **'I am my lover's and my lover is mine; he browses among the lilies'** (6:3). This is the same as what she said in 2:16, but in reverse order (see also 7:10). We have now moved from alienation to intimacy.

Sibbes sees in this verse mutual ownership, mutual love, mutual familiarity, mutual likeness, mutual care and mutual complacency. He also sees courage and resolution. He aptly quotes Isaiah 44:5 and Micah 4.5:

> One will say, 'I belong to the LORD';
>   another will call himself by the name of Jacob;
> still another will write on his hand, 'The LORD's',
>   and will take the name Israel.
>
> All the nations may walk
>   in the name of their gods;
> we will walk in the name of the LORD
>   our God for ever and ever.

He warns that 'It is but a delusion and self-flattery to say, "I am Christ's," when there is not the resolution to stand for Christ.' The believer says, 'I am not ashamed of my bargain, of the consent I have given him; I am his and I will be his.'

It is in fellowship with Christ that true love shows and expresses itself. We love Christ and he loves us at all times. Nothing can sever that bond. It is like marriage. 'What God has joined together, let man not separate' (Matt. 19:6; Mark 10:9). However, a marriage must be more than a piece of paper. It must be more than sharing the same bed. It must be marked by intimacy and by sharing, by closeness, confidence, friendship, partnership, togetherness. This is the fuel that enables a relationship to thrive. All this takes time — something that is often at a premium, especially when children come along and other pressures are there. Yet time must be found.

In the same way our relationship with Christ must be kept alive. We need to be in his presence. We must allow him to browse among the lilies. Is there time in your life for Christ? Do you welcome his leisurely visits?

The beauty of the bride

This leads on to a description of the beloved, another *wasf*. This is the man's second portrayal of the woman. There is some repetition, but there is a definite step up in the way he describes her. It points us again to the beauty of God's people, the church.

1. How attractive she is to the groom!

He begins by saying:

> **You are beautiful, my darling, as Tirzah,**
> **lovely as Jerusalem,**
> **majestic as troops with banners**
>
> (6:4).

The NIV translation almost masks the use of an identical phrase here and in verse 10 to form an *inclusio*: 'majestic as the stars in procession' is an alternative translation of **'majestic as troops with banners'**.

'Jerusalem' we know of. It is 'beautiful in its loftiness, the joy of the whole earth', is 'perfect in beauty', and 'glorious things are said' of it (Ps. 48:2; 50:2; 87:3). It points to the New Jerusalem. **'Tirzah'** means 'pleasantness' or 'sweetness'. It would become the capital city in Israel until King Omri built a new city, Samaria, to replace it. Archaeologists identify Tirzah with Tell el-Farah, six miles north of Shechem. The images are meant to convey ideas of beauty, of majesty and splendour. His other image is that of a majestic army with banners. This is how Christ sees his people — the noble army of the godly. The saints go marching in.

He says, **'Turn your eyes from me; they overwhelm me'** (6:5). He is amazed at what he sees. He is bashful in her presence. He is reserved, shy. Rather than describe her eyes, he describes their effect. Now to apply this to Christ and his church seems at first faintly ridiculous. Yet God delights to use these very human images to describe such things and, although we must never forget that all we have is from him, this is nevertheless the way that the Bible speaks. Too often our worship is man-centred and we do not think about things from God's side. This is certainly one element that we rarely consider at all.

How delightful she is to the groom! Some of the description from chapter 4 is more or less repeated. We have considered some of the traits here back in our sixth chapter. We shall not repeat those details here.

Her hair

> **Your hair is like a flock of goats**
> **descending from Mount Gilead**
>
> (6:5).

Her teeth

> **Your teeth are like a flock of sheep** [just shorn],
> **coming up from the washing.**
> **Each has its twin;**
> **not one of them is alone**
>
> (6:6).

194

Heavenly love

This time it is the more specific word for 'ewes', that is, females, rather than just **'sheep'** that is used.

Unlike the previous description, there is nothing here about her lips.

Her temples

> **Your temples behind your veil**
> **are like the halves of a pomegranate**

> (6:7).

These verses teach us not only to admire the beauty of a wife, but that Christ is full of delight in gazing upon his people. They remind us again of verses that have already been quoted (Zeph. 3:17; Ps. 147:11; 149:4).

Next we have more description.

2. Her nature is unique to him

> **Sixty queens there may be,**
> **and eighty concubines,**
> **and virgins beyond number;**
> **but my dove, my perfect one, is unique,**
> **the only daughter of her mother,**
> **the favourite of the one who bore her**

> (6:8-9).

To her he seems to be unique. Here it becomes clear that he sees her in very much the same way. He compares her with three categories of women — queens, concubines and virgins. These sound like different ranks within the royal harem and perhaps beyond. **'Queens'** are royal wives, those who would bear the king children and heirs. **'Concubines'** are royal wives of a lower status without the rights and privileges of queens. The reference to young women, or 'virgins', could be more general, or may refer to those who had been brought to the palace but had not yet gone in to the king. Whereas he is working downwards in point of rank, he is working upwards numerically. With all his experience of such things, Solomon is able to declare that this woman is head and shoulders above all potential rivals. In referring to her he uses the terms he had used in 5:2. She is her mother's chosen child, her special one.

3. Her nature is truly blessed

The maidens saw her and called her blessed;
the queens and concubines praised her.
Who is this that appears like the dawn,
fair as the moon, bright as the sun,
majestic as the stars in procession?

(6:9-10).

If we assume that **'the maidens'** here are 'the virgins' of 6:8, then we have the same three categories again. This time, he asserts, the women themselves can confirm that this woman is worthy of praise. The king may still be speaking in 6:10, but it is more likely to be the daughters of Jerusalem or the women mentioned in verses 8-9.

Whoever speaks, there is no disputing the answer to this rhetorical question. A four-part astronomical metaphor is used, suggesting freshness, height, purity and majesty. The dawn, the moon and the sun are referred to, suggesting that this second reference to an 'army with banners' is to the starry host. What an enviable position the church has! How truly blessed she is! What a privilege to be among that number!

On the horizontal plane, just as the portrait of the lover has lessons for husbands and prospective husbands, so similar remarks can be made with regard to the portrait of the beloved and wives, or prospective wives. They must remember how attractive and delightful they are to their husband, or intended husband. To him you are unique. You are in an enviable position indeed.

Where the bridegroom is to be found

Verses 11 and 12 stand apart in some ways from what has gone before. We consider them here, however, as they deal once more with the question of where the beloved's lover is to be found. In doing so, we shall ask three questions similar to those we have already asked. This again teaches us something about finding Christ when he appears to have gone from us.

1. Where is he to be found?

There is some debate over who speaks here, but it seems to be the lover who explains: **'I went down to the grove of nut trees'** (6:11). Those with an eye for this sort of thing are keen for us to see some sexual imagery in the reference to nuts. Without resorting to specifics, the very fact that the word **'grove'**, a term closely related to that for 'garden', is found here alerts us to the idea of intimate union in a parallel way to 6:2. Again we see, therefore, that Christ is found by his people in those moments of intimacy when he draws near — reading his Word or praying, hearing the Word preached, at the communion table, or in similar settings.

2. Why is he found there?

He continues by explaining why he had gone to that particular place. He had gone, he says, **'... to look at the new growth in the valley, to see if the vines had budded or the**

pomegranates were in bloom' (6:11). It was an exploratory trip. He wanted to see what was happening, how things were developing. Like a gardener or husbandman looking for signs of growth, he wanted to see the true state of affairs.

Again the spiritual point is that the Lord is one who is full of concern for us. Because of that he wants to probe us, to examine and test us:

> He observes the sons of men;
> > his eyes examine them.
> The LORD examines the righteous
>
> > > (Ps. 11:4).

He examines the righteous and probes their hearts and minds (see Jer. 20:12). Like a health inspector or a ticket inspector, he scrutinizes and checks with keen eyes. It can be irksome to us, as Job found:

> What is man that you make so much of him,
> > that you give him so much attention,
> that you examine him every morning
> > and test him every moment?
>
> > > (Job 7:17-18).

But it is in such intimacies that he is encountered, if we are awake to the fact.

3. What happened while he was there?

Next he tells us how, **'Before I realized it, my desire set me among the royal chariots of my people'** (6:12). This is a difficult verse and there are various translations of the latter part. For example:

My soul made me *like* the chariots of Amminadib (AV).

My soul set me *over* the chariots of my noble people (NASB).

My fancy set me in a chariot beside my prince ([N]RSV).

I found myself in my princely bed with my beloved one (NLT).

The likelihood of a personal name ('Amminadib') being intended is remote. 'Noble people' is probably to be preferred to 'noble person' or 'prince', so the idea surfaces of the speaker having suddenly found himself with the one(s) he loves. This echoes what has already been said above and underlines again the spiritual lesson that it is with his people that Christ is to be found. That determination on his part may sometimes leave us puzzled and trailing behind, but it is a key to understanding much that perplexes some of us in our Christian walk.

Longman warns that 'no one can speak with much certainty about' the interpretation of this verse, but perhaps an anecdote from the life of the great preacher C. H. Spurgeon may cast some light on the sort of logic at work here. The story I have in mind is from the second volume of his 'autobiography', as told by Mrs Spurgeon.

In the early days of the young couple's courtship a memorable incident occurred when Spurgeon was preaching one afternoon at a large hall called 'The Horns' in Kennington, just south of London. Spurgeon had asked his fiancée to accompany him and, after dining at her mother's house, they headed off in a hansom cab for the service. When they arrived Mrs Spurgeon says, 'I well remember trying to keep close by his side as we mingled with the mass of people thronging up the staircase. But, by the time we had reached the landing, he had forgotten my existence; the burden of the message he had to proclaim to that crowd of immortal souls was upon him, and he turned into the small side door where the officials were awaiting him, without for a moment realizing that I was left to struggle as best I could with the rough and eager throng around me.'

The preacher's desire was set on entering his chariot, that is, his pulpit. Mrs Spurgeon reacts in a similar way to the woman here. She continues: 'At first, I was utterly bewildered, and then, I am sorry to have to confess, I was *angry.* I at once returned home, and told my grief to my gentle mother, who tried to soothe my ruffled spirit, and bring me to a better frame of mind. She wisely reasoned that my chosen husband was no ordinary man, that his whole life was absolutely dedicated to God and His service, and that I must never, *never* hinder him by trying to put myself first in his heart.'

We then have a similar dénouement: 'Presently, after much good and loving counsel, my heart grew soft, and I saw I had been very foolish and wilful; and then a cab drew up at the door, and dear Mr Spurgeon came running into the house, in great excitement, calling, "Where's Susie? I have been searching for her everywhere, and cannot find her; has she come back by herself?" My dear mother went to him, took him aside, and told him all the truth; and I think, when he realized the state of things, she had to soothe him also, for he was so innocent at heart of having offended me in any way, that he must have felt I had done him an injustice in thus doubting him. At last, mother came to fetch me to him, and I went downstairs. Quietly he let me tell him how indignant I had felt, and then he repeated mother's little lesson, assuring me of his deep affection for me, but pointing out that, before all things, he was *God's servant,* and I must be prepared to yield my claims to His.'

The illustration does not quite fit, of course, but gives the idea of an overwhelming sense of need to be among God's people and illustrates how that desire may at times conflict with undoubted loyalties to a dearly loved individual. Something of this sort is going on here in the Song. Mrs Spurgeon concludes by saying, 'What a delightfully cosy tea we three had together that evening, and how sweet was the calm in our hearts after the storm...!'

She also hints at the way the incident deepened their love for each other, a love 'which can look a misunderstanding in the face till it melts away and vanishes, as a morning cloud before the ardent glances of the sun'.

To sum up

This chapter reminds us of Christ — his outstanding nature, nobility, tenderness, the richness and profusion that characterize him, the fragrace of his words, his gracious works, strength, splendid appearance, sweetness and loveliness. Is he your Lover and Friend? If he is, give thanks for such a perfect Saviour. If you do not know him, consider his portrait and put your faith in him today.

As for the church — how attractive and delightful she is to the Groom! To him her nature is unique and she is truly blessed indeed. When we lose connection with the Lord it is in the flow of the life of the church, corporately and individually, that we make connection again with our head, who is Christ.

The portrait of the Lover is a perfect model for husbands and prospective husbands. Are we noble, tender, fragrant, gracious, strong and sweet? Are our looks, words and actions towards our wives what they should be? Wives, remember too how attractive and delightful you are to your husband. To him your nature is unique. If you have a man who truly cares for you, you are blessed indeed.

11.
Completeness: The nature of true love in its maturity

Please read Song of Songs 6:13 – 8:4

We have considered the courtship and marriage between the king and his beloved and the falling out and separation that threatened their relationship, with the beautiful reconciliation that followed. In this next section we see the relationship in its maturity. Again there are lessons for us to learn about a covenant relationship on both the horizontal and vertical planes. We learn about mature married love and about a mature Christian relationship with the Lord Jesus Christ.

These verses are full of instruction. The pattern is as follows:

Shulammite	Friends	Solomon
—	6:13a?	—
6:13b?	—	—
—	—	7:1-9a
7:9b – 8:4	—	—

Who speaks in 6:13 is debatable. More than one person is speaking in the first part of the verse. I take it that once again this is the daughters of Jerusalem. They say, **'Come back, come back, O Shulammite; come back, come back, that**

we may gaze on you!' It is probably the woman who,
referring to herself in the third person, then asks, **'Why
would you gaze on the Shulammite as on the dance of
Mahanaim?'**

Although we have used it extensively in this commentary,
this is the only occurrence in the whole book of the term
'Shulammite'. How are we to understand it? A reference to
a pagan goddess (as some have suggested) seems highly
unlikely; one to Shunem in Galilee is possible. It is probably
best understood as a feminine form of Solomon, suggesting a
double reference to peace (*shalom*). I take the view that the
Shulammite is the woman referred to throughout the book.

The repeated appeal to **'come back'** may be a simple
request for the woman to turn towards the speakers, or it may
have something to do with her twirling movement detectable
in 7:1. Perhaps they feel they are losing her to her lover. She
replies with diffidence. Why should they want to look at her
like a crowd gathering to watch two armies fight, or like
someone entertaining the troops (*mahanaim*)? She still has
an attractive modesty about her. This verse sets the scene for
what follows in chapter 7. (In Hebrew Bibles 6:13 is the first
verse of chapter 7.)

Mature husbandly love — observations and desires

The institution of marriage continues to be under a great deal
of pressure in many places today. It is not simply that marriages often fail to work out after a short while, but in some
cases there are divorces after ten, twenty and sometimes even
thirty or forty years of marriage. There seems to be a wide-
spread failure to understand that one of the great things about
marriage is that, ideally, it gets better and better as it goes on.
It is foolish and naïve to think that after just a few years a
couple will have experienced all the joys that there are to

know in married life. Perhaps the fact that so many seem to think like this is one of the factors that make the divorce rate so high. On the other hand, it could be the other way around. Maybe expectation is high but realization low. Marriage is meant to be a developing thing, a growing and maturing union, a relationship of increasing intimacy that gets better and better as the years go by.

Sadly, it is not always like that. Too often couples confess that they have grown apart. Jay Adams suggests that a good question to put to couples with troubles is: 'Has there been growth, decline, or a plateauing of your marriage relationship during the last six months?' This is a good question for any couple to ask.

Now if it is true that a marriage relationship should be dynamic and growing, how much more should it be so of the covenant relationship between the believer and his Lord, the relationship that marriage so powerfully but imperfectly reflects! Conversion really is only the beginning. How much more there is in store, even before we reach heaven! As Isaac Watts wrote so long ago:

The hill of Zion yields
A thousand sacred sweets
Before we reach the heavenly fields
Or walk the golden streets.

In chapter 7 we have yet another *wasf*. At first sight, some verses may seem rather familiar. If we look more carefully, we shall see development and change. Here we are observing the lovers at a more mature stage in their relationship — after the courtship and the marriage, after certain setbacks and reconciliations that have served ultimately to strengthen the relationship. When you read the opening verses of chapter 7 your mind immediately goes back to the portrayal of the bride that the groom gave on their wedding night in chapter 4. There are definite affinities between the two passages, even repetitions, but also certain differences and additions. No doubt the writer follows the same pattern to facilitate a comparison of the descriptions. We immediately notice that this second passage is a fuller, more sensual, even erotic, delineation of the woman.

Things have moved on from the wedding night. Then he saw that she was perfect and so gave a sevenfold description of her. Now he sees it even more clearly, so this time his list contains *ten* different items! Ten is another number indicating fulness and completeness, but even greater than seven. This is also the same number of items as in the description she gives of him in chapter 5. Christ enables his own to grow ever more lovely by letting them become ever more like him.

1. Observations typical of mature husbandly love

Previously the bridegroom began with the woman's face and did not go much further than that. Here he begins with her feet and works his way up to her hair. Perhaps it is 6:13 that prompts the decision to begin there. She may well be dancing. It is also fair to note that, as true love develops, it sees more and more things to admire. Things once considered insignificant are now seen in a better light. Solomon is here answering the question as to why so much attention should be paid to the Shulammite. The description is intimate and personal, not lustful, perverted or disrespectful.

Her feet

'How beautiful your sandalled feet, O prince's daughter!' (7:1). Perhaps, as has already been suggested, the beloved is dancing, or at least turning — giving a twirl! Hence we begin with her sandalled feet. As we have seen before, this book is not shy about the use of beauty aids and fashion accessories.

Sandals, shoes and boots are familiar aids to style which for some women can become an obsession. The vast collection of footwear gathered by Imelda Marcos, wife of the former Filipino president, became a byword for excess. Feet generally come in the less presentable category of body parts, especially if accompanied by thick ankles, so any help from well-crafted footwear is usually appreciated. Raised heels, pointed toes, strategic gaps and pretty patterns are all utilized. In the Apocrypha it says that when Judith seduced Holofernes 'her sandal ravished his eyes' (Judith 16:9).

The king uses a term of the highest respect and intimacy when addressing the woman — **'O prince's daughter,'** he says, or 'Noble daughter'. This reminds us of the exalted state of those who trust in Jesus Christ. They are not left to go barefoot but are given sandals, as it were, just as in the desert God provided for the Israelites so that their shoes never wore out: 'During the forty years that I led you through the desert, your clothes did not wear out, nor did the sandals on your feet' (Deut. 29:5). More than that, he enables us to have 'feet fitted with the readiness that comes from the gospel of peace' (Eph. 6:15).

Like the Shulammite, believers are nobodies by nature. Why should anyone be interested in us? However, we have become daughters of the Prince of peace, the one whom 'God exalted … to his own right hand as Prince and Saviour that he might give repentance and forgiveness of sins to Israel' (Acts 5:31). We are members of the royal family, by the grace of God:

> He raises the poor from the dust
> and lifts the needy from the ash heap;
> he seats them with princes,
> with the princes of their people
>
> (Ps. 113:7-8).

Her legs

'**Your graceful legs are like jewels, the work of a crafts-man's hands**' (7:1). This follows on from the reference to the feet. It is her thighs or hips, even her buttocks, which he has in mind rather than the whole leg. As she either dances, or merely sways and swings her hips, he notices this. This whole area of a woman's body is held to be most erotic, as its shape is exceptionally feminine. The word translated '**graceful**' really means 'rounded', or 'curvy', as we might say today. The '**jewels**' could be rings. Perhaps he is think-ing not only of the shapeliness of her upper legs but also of their movement — like that of a jewelled pendant swinging back and forth in time to music. The image is intended to depict the smoothness of her legs, rather than suggesting that they sparkle. A craftsman has been at work to bring this about. It is God who makes beautiful legs and he is the one who enables believers to stand, and to dance with joy too, to his glory.

Her navel

'**Your navel is a rounded goblet that never lacks blended wine**' (7:2). And so up to her navel. Common enough in Western society today, women's navels were for many years banished from films and TV. The metaphor of '**blended wine**' does not need to be pursued relentlessly, although a '**rounded goblet**' is evocative of a woman's navel. Wine here stands simply for pleasure. Some observers detect a modern preference for vertical navels whereas in the past a rounded navel was thought to be most attractive, as here. Whether or not the king can see her navel is unclear. Perhaps the fashion for crop tops was riding high at the time, or the couple were in private and he looked. If it was covered he simply imagines it. By likening it to a glass of wine he suggests that she is like a satisfying drink to him — quenching thirst, giving strength, inducing joy. This is how husbands should see their wives and how Christ sees his church.

Her waist

'Your waist is a mound of wheat encircled by lilies' (7:2). The picture is of wheat stacked up as it would be at harvest time and encircled with cornflowers, or something similar. He is probably thinking of the slimness of her waist, her svelte figure, and perhaps the flowers embroidered on her dress. Beneath her waist, of course, lies her womb. Grain and wine are often spoken of together in Scripture (e.g. Ps. 4:7, Isa. 62:8) and symbolize fruitfulness and nourishment. There is an abundance of both food and drink, then. This speaks to us of the way that Christ sees the church he has provided for and is satisfied in it.

Her breasts

'Your breasts are like two fawns, twins of a gazelle' (7:3). This is the same phrase as he used in 4:5 (though the spelling of one word in the Hebrew is slightly different). As we noted then, a description of a woman's breasts is not something we would normally speak about, but this is an intimate moment. Breasts speak not only of softness and tenderness, but also, like the previous image, of provision and abundance.

Her neck

'Your neck is like an ivory tower' (7:4). This is a variation on the phrase used in 4:4. It may seem a strange description, but he is thinking of the smoothness, the length and strength, and probably also the whiteness, of her neck. Believers, like ivory, are costly and precious to the Saviour and strong in him.

Her eyes

'Your eyes are the pools of Heshbon by the gate of Bath Rabbim' (7:4). This is similar to the image she uses to describe him in 5:12. **'Heshbon'** was an old Amorite capital on the eastern side of the Dead Sea. The reference sounds proverbial but **'Bath Rabbim'** means 'daughter of many' or 'daughter of nobles'. The woman's moist eyes are likened to the pools there — large, deep, clear, tranquil and still. Eyes are often mentioned when we think of love. Christ looks into our eyes and he sees us. He looks with complacency if he sees his own reflection and knows we are looking to him.

Her nose

'Your nose is like the tower of Lebanon looking towards Damascus' (7:4). Again this seems a little strange to our ears. George Jabet's *Notes on noses* (published in 1852) says that some consider the nose 'too ridiculous an organ' to speak of. If they are willing to discuss it most people prefer a very small one, but a long one can be just as beautiful. Here is a nose that is straight, not crooked — a strong feature. Straightness and vigilance are further qualities that the Lord looks for in us and admires when he sees.

Her head

'Your head crowns you like Mount Carmel' (7:5). As Mount Carmel dominates the north-west of Canaan near the Mediterranean with its grandeur, so this woman's head caps it all. Carmel was high and was marked by fruitfulness. It is the place where Elijah would one day triumph over the prophets of Baal. Perhaps we should think of the way that Christ looks to us to stand up for him in a dignified manner, and to be fruitful and faithful. When he sees that, he is delighted.

Her hair

'Your hair is like royal tapestry; the king is held captive by its tresses' (7:5). Her hair has a richness and a beauty all its own. It is silky, smooth and full of colour. He imagines himself tied down by her tresses, so drawn is he to this aspect of her beauty. Gledhill quotes Alexander Pope and Thomas Carew, who make similar observations about a woman's hair:

> Fair tresses man's imperial race ensnare,
> And beauty draws us with a single hair.

Or:

> Those curious locks so aptly twined
> Whose every hair a soul doth bind.

Longfellow's 'Saga of King Olaf' says, 'Not ten yoke of oxen have the power to draw us like a woman's hair.'

A woman's long hair is her glory (1 Cor. 11:15). Note here the regal reference once again — **'royal tapestry'** (literally 'purple' — perhaps there is an indigo hue to her hair, whether natural or artificial.) As believers, we find it hard to believe that Christ should show such interest in us, but he does. Think of how he reacted to the amazing faith of the centurion. We read that he 'was astonished and said to those following him, "I tell you the truth, I have not found anyone in Israel with such great faith"' (Matt. 8:10). So Jesus seeks such virtues in us who believe. Do we remember

just how highly we are regarded by Christ? We must realize
how great his love for us is.

2. *Desires typical of mature husbandly love*

In 7:6 the king sums up with: **'How beautiful you are and
how pleasing, O love, with your delights!'** To God his
people are *Hephzibah* — the Lord delights in us. Then he
goes on to use another picture: **'Your stature is like that of
the palm, and your breasts like clusters of fruit'** (7:7).

The word for palm tree is *tamar*. The very word acquired
sexual overtones, as the name Tamar belonged to Judah's
daughter-in-law (Gen. 38) and Amnon's half-sister (2 Sam.
13) whose sad stories both concern sexual relationships. The
point here, though, is that this woman stands tall and steady,
slender, graceful, elegant, pleasing to the eye. Her breasts are
like fruit — dates perhaps — growing high on a palm tree.
Fruitfulness is a common picture of productivity in the
Christian life. Think of how Jesus uses it in his parable of the
sower and his allegory of the vine.

Finally, Solomon uses two more striking and sensual
images to describe his desire for this woman, for his wife.

He thinks of embracing and caressing her

> **I said, 'I will climb the palm tree;**
> **I will take hold of its fruit.'**
> **May your breasts be like the clusters of the vine...**
> **(7:8).**

Just as a man may hug a tree in order to climb it, so the
husband pictures himself enfolding his beloved in an intimate embrace and coming ever nearer to her fruit. He then
speaks of taking hold of her fruit — caressing her, touching

her breasts in particular. Think of holding a lovely bunch of succulent dates or grapes.

Like all females of the mammalian species, most women are able to produce milk from their breasts to feed babies and young children. The Bible makes references to this. Job 24:9 speaks of 'the fatherless child ... snatched from the breast; the infant of the poor... seized for a debt'. David trusted in God at his 'mother's breast' (Ps. 22:9). Isaiah 49:15 is famous. It begins: 'Can a mother forget the baby at her breast and have no compassion on the child she has borne?' Isaiah also speaks of 'children weaned from their milk ... those just taken from the breast' and, metaphorically, of drinking 'the milk of nations', of being 'nursed at royal breasts' and of 'comforting breasts' (Isa. 28:9; 60:16; 66:11). Joel 2:16 also mentions 'those nursing at the breast'. Jesus himself speaks of a time when people will say, 'Blessed are the barren women, the wombs that never bore and the breasts that never nursed!' (Luke 23:29).

On the other hand, there are passages that refer to the sexual attractiveness of breasts, which comes from their ideal softness and smoothness, their shapeliness and femininity. Apart from what we find here in the Song of Solomon, two passages in particular spring to mind:

> May your fountain be blessed,
>   and may you rejoice in the wife of your youth.
> A loving doe, a graceful deer —
>   may her breasts satisfy you always,
>   may you ever be captivated by her love
>
> (Prov. 5:18-19).

> They became prostitutes in Egypt, engaging in pros-
> titution from their youth. In that land their breasts were
> fondled and their virgin bosoms caressed... So you
> longed for the lewdness of your youth, when in Egypt

your bosom was caressed and your young breasts fondled (Ezek. 23:3,21).

One can understand the frustration of women like Germaine Greer, who says that they are only 'admired for as long as they show no sign of their function', but it is facile to suggest that what at times approaches something of an obsession with female breasts in the Western world is a misunderstanding of what they are for. Their sexual appeal is not in doubt. Having said that, what is lost in the eddies of silicone implantation and the currents of pornographic representation is the chaste and uncorrupted way that the Bible deals with this matter, including the binding of the subject to its appropriate marital context. Such considerations should direct the way a man thinks of his wife.

He thinks of her intimate kisses

'**[May] the fragrance of your breath [be] like apples, and your mouth like the best wine'** (7:8-9). This continues the image of fruit and recalls the reference to wine back in 7:2. The word translated '**breath**' is difficult. The reference could be to 'the breath of your nose'. Nose-rubbing is not a practice confined to Inuit peoples of the frozen north! The suggestion that we translate it as 'nipple' makes no sense in connection with '**fragrance**'. The word '**mouth**' refers to the palate, the inner mouth. He thinks of a deep kiss. Clearly the caressing, or hugging, and the kissing go together, and where the two things are divorced there is undoubtedly something amiss.

There should be a fragrance about God's people. In our singing and speaking, and in all our lives, there should be something of the aroma of Christ: 'Let your conversation be always full of grace, seasoned with salt, so that you may know how to answer everyone' (Col. 4:6). 'Do not let any unwholesome talk come out of your mouths, but only what is helpful for building others up according to their needs, that it may benefit those who listen' (Eph. 4:29). Our prayers and praises should be like sweet fragrance rising to heaven, like refreshing wine to our God.

And so they lie there, arms entwined, embracing.

A mature response to husbandly love

Then, from the end of 7:9 on into 8:4, we have the Shulammite's response. How does she react? Is it 'Not tonight dear' or 'Oh you are a soppy one!'? Not at all. She responds appropriately. As he sleeps, she speaks of her love for him. We note three characteristics in her attitude.

1. Mature commitment

First, she takes up his image of kisses being like wine in the mouth and she says, **'May the wine go straight to my lover, flowing gently over lips and teeth'** (7:9). Then she continues: **'I belong to my lover, and his desire is for me'** (7:10). We have had similar phrases before. They occur in 2:16 and 6:3. If you look at these three phrases carefully you will observe evidence of a deepening love and security.

In 2:16 she puts her possession of her beloved Solomon first and his possession of her second: 'My beloved is mine and I am his.' The second time, she reverses the order, suggesting a greater sense of security: 'I am my lover's and my lover is mine' (6:3). Here she once again begins by stating that she belongs to him, then goes on to express his desire for her, and does not even mention her possession of him: 'I belong to my lover, and his desire is for me.' The word she uses for **'desire'** is a very strong one. It only occurs here and in Genesis 3:16; 4:7. How great are our desires for Christ?

2. *Willing desires to see love renewed*

As her lover wakes, she speaks again. She has a plan:

> **Come, my lover, let us go to the countryside,**
> **let us spend the night in the villages.**
> **Let us go early to the vineyards**
> **to see if the vines have budded,**
> **if their blossoms have opened,**
> **and if the pomegranates are in bloom —**
> **there I will give you my love**
>
> (7:11-12).

She wants them to go on a trip, to spend a night away from all the busyness. 'We need to get away,' she says. 'We need to spend some time alone. We need to be out and away from all these distractions, disruptions and disturbances.' We have already observed the connection between lovemaking and the countryside (literally here, 'the field'). This reference and the phrase **'spend the night'** make quite clear what she has in mind.

This is how mature love responds. It is not only young lovers who need time alone, but those who have been married for some time too. It is difficult with children, especially as they grow older and are around for more of the day, but somehow husbands and wives have to be alone together. Many have benefited from some of the work of Americans Gary and Maria Ezzo. One of the Ezzos' ideas is what I believe they call 'sofa time'. The idea is that when dad comes in from work his children need to realize that his number one priority is to spend some time on the sofa talking to mum. He will come to them in a short while, but first there has to be time for his wife. Whether or not Christian couples practise Ezzo-type 'sofa time' is immaterial. What matters is that they realize the importance of having time for each other. When a Christian couple decide on a day or two's break away from it all (without the kids!) they may feel they are being a little selfish. However, if they do it honestly before God they are in fact seizing an opportunity to replenish and enhance their relationship, something that tends not only to their own good but to that of many others too.

Now if this is so in marriage, how much more so when it comes to intimacy with Christ! It is a struggle sometimes, but, with what American preacher Al Martin once described as 'sanctified viciousness', we must guard our times of being alone with the Lord to pray and to read his Word. This is absolutely vital. Are we finding the time for such things? The idea of being up early (**'let us go early'**) is perhaps a clue to this. Maybe **'spend the night'** has something to say too (see Luke 6:12).

Note too the idea of looking for evidence of growth: **'to see if the vines have budded, if their blossoms have opened, and if the pomegranates are in bloom'**. Love has to be articulated if it is real love. If we really love the Lord, that love will find expression. We need to find time for that — corporately, when God's people gather together, in our families and when we are alone. Surely Mark 6:31 supports the idea of getting away from it all to be alone with the Lord? The desire of the Christian to be on his own with God should be so that there he may give the Lord his love.

The wife continues:

> **The mandrakes send out their fragrance,**
> **and at our door is every delicacy,**
> **both new and old,**
> **that I have stored up for you, my lover**

(7:13).

She has it all prepared. Mandrake plants are part of the potato family and produce long leaves and sweet-smelling flowers. The fruit is sometimes referred to as the love apple. They have long been renowned for their aphrodisiac qualities and power to aid conception — probably due to the appearance of their phallic, or humanoid, root shapes, or perhaps because of their narcotic effect. You may remember their role in the story of Jacob's family: one time 'during wheat harvest', Leah's son 'Reuben went out into the fields and found some mandrake plants, which he brought to his mother'. Rachel then asked Leah for some of Reuben's mandrakes, only to be told that the price for them was the opportunity for Leah to sleep with Jacob, something that she had not enjoyed for a while. This led to the birth of Jacob's fifth son, Issachar, and a new lease of life for the relationship between Leah and Jacob (Gen. 30:14-16). Whether mandrakes can achieve anything quite so spectacular in a more conventional way is debatable. Their mention here, however, shows that this woman has everything prepared.

Along with the mandrakes, there is **'every delicacy'**, that is every fruit. I suppose today we might speak of flowers and chocolates, or perhaps the romantic candlelit meal. The plenty and the variety and the phrase **'new and old'** (a figure of speech called a merism in which two extremes stand for the whole range) are all very evocative in both the horizontal and vertical spheres.

Jesus says, 'Therefore every teacher of the law who has been instructed about the kingdom of heaven is like the owner of a house who brings out of his storeroom new treasures as well as old' (Matt. 13:52). This verse is usually taken to be a description of the best sort of Christian teaching. Using the image of a meal, Jesus says that the way to teach is to bring out of one's storeroom 'new treasures as well as old', things already in the house and other things newly provided for the occasion, old standbys and new recipes too. We can think of this in terms of making judicious use of both Old and New Testaments, or things from one's past and one's present experience and study. The right sort of teacher is always fresh, yet also willing and able to make good use of older spiritual treasures in Scripture or from Christian history.

What keeps a marriage fresh? It is that excellent mixture of the familiar and the new. A marriage can grow stale as the years go by. Familiarity can breed contempt. That is why some think the answer is to start up again with someone else. 'Trade her in for a new model,' as the chauvinist might joke. Thus we see men in their fifties and sixties starting all over again with a new wife and a young family. Such radical departures are not necessary, however. Rather there needs to be a right mix of new and old — the same couple, doing at least some of the same things, but branching out into new areas, employing new ideas, new approaches, new ways.

Something similar can be said about our relationship with Christ. It is a fascinating mix of old and new. It is easy to become hackneyed in our praying, dry in our Bible reading, weary in other aspects of our spiritual lives, but the right mixture of old and new will help us to avoid this particular pitfall.

3. Eager longing for ever greater intimacy

Finally, in the opening verses of chapter 8, the woman speaks of her desire for increasing intimacy with her lover. Customs differ from society to society, of course, but in many Near and Far-Eastern cultures, even today, displays of affection in public between husbands and wives are taboo. The only people you see kissing in public are brothers and sisters. That appears to be why she says here:

If only you were to me like a brother,
   who was nursed at my mother's breasts!
Then, if I found you outside,
   I would kiss you,
   and no one would despise me

                                                            (8:1).

Back in 4:9,12 he had spoken of her as his sister. Here she wishes that he was her little brother. The reference to her mother's breasts may be intended to be erotic, but does not have to be. The point is that she would like to be free to kiss him just when she wished, and even though they are married, as every couple knows, for various reasons that is not always possible. To speak of her fantasizing here, as Elizabeth Huwiler does, is probably unhelpful. Imagination is certainly important in lovemaking — the whole book supports that idea — but to fantasize is to let the imagination run riot in an unreal world. It can be a minefield. Christian couples will wisely avoid stepping into it.

She goes on:

I would lead you
   and bring you to my mother's house —
   she who has taught me.
I would give you spiced wine to drink,
   the nectar of my pomegranates

                                                            (8:2).

This is another picture of great intimacy, the intimacy that she longs for with him, and that all husbands and wives ought to long to have with one another. Now they are married, she is quite bold about leading him, yet only in the context of giving something to him. Sometimes young Christian men have rather wooden ideas of male headship in marriage. A verse like this suggests that it is a little more complex than the man saying, 'I make all the decisions round here.'

The reference to her mother again, **'she who has taught me'**, is interesting. Some want, without warrant, to emend that phrase to make it match 3:4. There is certainly something very special about the relationship between a mother and her children, especially mother and daughter. That relationship is not lost when a woman marries. Rather it should be enhanced. All that the mother has taught her daughter now comes into play. Mothers-in-law have traditionally been the butt of music-hall comedy, but that ought not to be. From personal experience I can say that there is something particularly good about being with your wife in her mother's house. There you are face to face with the original model and setting, the source of much of what attracted you to your wife in the first place. There is a school of thought that says that when choosing a wife it is a good idea, where possible, to observe the mother with the thought that 'This is how she will be twenty years on.' There is something in that.

Some see **'mother's house'** as a euphemism for sexual activity. Certainly in the latter half of the verse we are in the bedroom and the language is very sensuous. 'Sanctified eroticism', Henry Morris calls it. It springs from the happiness of not only being with her lover, but in the safety of the parental home, with all its happy memories.

'My mother ... who has taught me' could also be a reference to wisdom. She is going to instruct him in what she knows about making love. If so, this reinforces the point made earlier about women taking the lead. Certainly there is no biblical reason for supposing that it is the man who is always to be the initiator in these things.

At last, she says, **'His left arm is under my head and his right arm embraces me'** (8:3). Apart from a very minor difference, this repeats 2:6. Here they are alone, intimately embracing, making love in complete bliss, just as it should be.

The warning again about the need for patience

We close with a consideration of 8:4: **'Daughters of Jerusa-lem I charge you: Do not arouse or awaken love until it so desires.'**

This repeats the warnings found in 2:7 and 3:5. It is strengthened this time, however, by shortening it (there is no oath) and using a stronger negative. The picture that we have described above is one that is so wonderful that we are immediately attracted to it, and there is the danger of then wanting so much to experience it that we try to bring it about immediately. However, we must see that such a relationship comes about only with great patience and perseverance.

Those who are children or young teenagers need to concentrate first on growing up to be marriageable men and women. Your mother will probably be a great help to you in this, especially if she is a Christian. If for some reason she cannot provide such guidance, then look to some other godly adult. You do not need to worry at all about marriage at present.

As for an older person who is still single but would like to be married, you know that there is no point in marrying just anyone. Great care and consideration, much patience and prayer are necessary. That is true especially in courtship.

Even when we are married, we must see that the close-ness that we have seen in other couples does not come overnight. Marriage is hard work. There is need for perse-verance and persistence, for fresh starts and new beginnings and an increasing delight in, and devotion towards, one another.

Something similar can be said about intimacy with Christ. That does not come instantly either, despite what some schools of thought claim. Growing in grace is something that again demands hard work, serious toil, unrelenting slog and, with it, much patience and persistence. If we walk in the right way, the Lord Jesus will increasingly delight in us. We in turn ought to respond with ever deeper and constantly growing desires for a close walk with him. Things ought to get better and better; we ought to draw closer and closer to the Lord Jesus Christ each day.

To sum up

A marriage should grow, getting better year on year. As it develops, true love sees more and more in the other person to admire. Married women are to be marked by mature commitment, willing desires to see love renewed and eager longings for increasing intimacy. For this to happen time together is vital, as is a balanced use of old and new.

Mothers-in-law are allies, not enemies. Christian mothers are a great help to young people in growing up to be marriageable adults. Singles who would like to be married know the need for great care and patience. Even after marriage, closeness does not come overnight. Marriage is hard work.

Conversion is only the beginning of the Christian life. There is much yet in store, even before heaven. Though by nature we are nobodies, the Lord provides for us. By grace we belong to the royal family. We are precious to him and strong in him. He looks on us with complacency where he sees his own reflection and knows we are looking to him. As believers, we find it hard to believe that Christ is interested in us, but he is. He wants us to have an intimate relationship with him. There should be an aroma of Christ about us in all our lives.

Guard your times alone with the Lord. If we really love him, our love will find expression. We need to find time for that. Intimacy with him does not come overnight. To grow in grace demands hard work. Walk in the right way, making judicious use of things old and new, and the Lord will increasingly delight in you. Draw closer and closer to him each day.

12.
Continuing: How to commence, continue and complete a loving covenant relationship

Please read Song of Songs 8:5-15

This is as good as it will get,
You won't improve on this —
Your wife, your kids, the table set,
All giving God due praise.

King David thought Uriah's wife
Could make him feel brand new
And maybe there are times in life
When you think like that too.

But we must see that this is true,
You can't improve on this —
To have your family there with you,
All praising God — that's bliss!

These lines by Darby Gray were prompted by a series of messages on Christian marriage given to a group of ministers by Derek Thomas. Dr Thomas began by recalling a basic truth. Genuine earthly bliss is to be sought and found in a

God-ordered family, not the adulteress's bed — a reminder we all need to hear from time to time.

This is an appropriate thought to have in mind as we come to the very last section of the Song of Songs. Again we are considering what we can learn from the love story between King Solomon and his beloved. Once more we are considering their covenant relationship of love and seeking lessons on both horizontal and vertical planes.

Previously, we have had sometimes quite lengthy speeches, fairly easy to identify, mainly from the bride and her lover. In the book's closing verses a series of speeches come in rapid succession from various speakers. These are not always easy to assign. The NIV is probably right to identify six different speeches — three from the beloved, two from the friends (in the first part of 8:5 and 8:8-9) and one from the lover (8:13), as set out in the table below:

Shulammite	Friends	Solomon
—	8:5a	—
8:5b-7	—	—
—	8:8-9	—
8:10-12	—	—
—	—	8:13
8:14	—	—

However we divide up the speeches, we gain the impression of a coming together and a certain concluding unity. Longman speaks very highly of verses 5-7, noting that they are 'the only place in the Song that really steps back and reflects on the nature of love itself'. The whole passage through to the end teaches four very useful things.

Key elements in a loving covenant relationship

We start at the beginning of 8:5 with what must be something resembling the chorus in Greek drama — a group providing comment or observation. By means of a question, they draw attention to the beloved walking along, on the arm of her lover, coming up out of the wilds of the desert. They ask, **'Who is this coming up from the desert leaning on her lover?'**

Back in 3:6 we had a similar enquiry. Here the question is asked again, and this time we see that still, at this more mature period in their marriage, the bride is leaning on her husband. She puts all her weight on him. This is a powerful picture not only of marriage, but also of the relationship between Christ and his church. There are three things to note in particular:

1. They are together.
2. They are leaving the desert behind.
3. The beloved is leaning on her lover.

This is how it should be in a marriage. Songwriter Sir Paul McCartney claims to have been in the company of his first wife Linda practically every day of their lives together. They were hardly ever separated. No doubt this was in part what lay behind the apparent strength of that marriage. This is not to say that husbands and wives have to be physically in one another's company twenty-four hours a day, seven days a week, for the marriage to work. (That certainly was not the case with John and Mary Newton, mentioned later on in this chapter.) However, they do need to spend time together and to be together in other respects too. When a husband and wife are apart for long periods, as happens today when, for instance, husbands are working or studying in another town or even another country, an inevitable strain is placed on the couple. Some of today's biggest problems, such as unfaithfulness in general and AIDS in particular, are greatly exacerbated by this practice. Paul's advice to couples in 1 Corinthians 7:5, though arising in a different context, applies here: 'Do not deprive each other except by mutual consent and for a time, so that you may devote yourselves to prayer. Then come together again so that Satan will not tempt you because of your lack of self-control.'

Always a marriage should be going forward, and where there are barren patches — dry and fruitless times — then they must be left behind by the grace of God. Going over old ground, especially when it has been parched and unfruitful, is not going to help anyone. Again the context is different but Paul's words, this time to the Philippians, have an application here: 'Forgetting what is behind and straining towards what is ahead, I press on towards the goal to win the prize for which God has called me heavenwards in Christ Jesus' (Phil. 3:13-14).

The normal pattern is that the woman should lean on the man, not the other way round. This leaning suggests trust and ease on one side, encouragement and acceptance on the other. Although in one sense it works both ways, a husband should endeavour to be a source of strength and support to his wife. She is to be treated (as Peter exhorts in 1 Peter 3:7) 'as the weaker partner'. Ideally, the way forward in marriage is to leave the desert behind, pressing on to heaven, to stay together, and for the wife to lean more than ever on her husband in Christ. Problems come in a marriage when there is no progress, no togetherness, or when either the husband fails to shoulder his responsibilities as he ought to, or the wife looks elsewhere for support.

When we come to the relationship between Christ and his church, it is certain that we must always lean on him. He is the one who upholds us and leads us out of the desert and on to heaven as together we share his easy yoke. It is a question to ponder: 'Who is this coming up from the desert leaning on her lover?' It is the Lord Jesus Christ and his church, the people of God, heading for home in the company of its one Lord and Saviour, Jesus Christ. Is Christ leading you out of the desert? Are you with him? Are you leaning ever more heavily upon him? That is the way forward for the Christian. This is how we must go forward as individuals, as married couples and families, and as a company of his people.

How to continue a loving covenant relationship

> And I will love thee still, my dear,
> Till a' the seas gang dry:
> Till a' the seas gang dry, my dear,
> And the rocks melt with the sun;
> I will love thee still, my dear
> When the sands of life shall run.

Robert Burns, it seems, was better at expressing such sentiments than living them out. Even the best of lovers may falter over the long haul. We have seen the basic principle involved in going on in a covenant relationship of love. What can we also learn about what we need to do in order to carry on? How do we keep on keeping on? We can say three things in particular.

1. Remember how it all began

The beloved speaks next (or perhaps the lover?):

> **Under the apple tree I roused you;**
> **there your mother conceived you,**
> **there she who was in labour gave you birth**
>
> (8:5).

The imagery could be taken as a reference to sexual activity. There is something striking, almost transcendent, about the very fact of procreation. By this act, one generation begets another, having itself been reproduced by the previous generation. Here, however, it is probably the case that one of them is recalling their first meeting. One is sleeping under an apple tree, when he or she is awoken by the other. Bearing in mind the spiritual application that we believe is appropriate to this portion of Scripture, it is tempting to assume that the lover is speaking. It is appropriate to think of the woman as being asleep — exhausted perhaps, certainly dead to his charms. Then he comes to her, wakes her and she is, as it were, conceived and born. That was the beginning of life.

If you are a Christian you may not be exactly sure when you were converted, but you can at least probably remember the first time you were really sure that you were, or when you first awoke to your spiritual situation. Such a memory is precious and should be recalled. There you were, dead to God and to life in Christ, when the Lord came and woke you. He gently raised you and you were born again (see Ezek. 16:4-6).

However, having said all this, it is more likely that it is the beloved speaking. She has referred to him before as an apple tree and it may well be that she is speaking of him again using this term. Otherwise she simply has in mind a fruit tree and all that this image evokes with regard to romance. Maybe we can think of Eve finding Adam asleep under a tree in Eden following her creation. Perhaps that event is in mind here. Spiritually speaking, the woman is recalling, as she has before, the coming of Christ into this world and her discovery of him by the grace of God. It is good when we remember, as best we can, how it all began. How excited we were to discover Christ, asleep as it were! How eager we were to wake him and receive his blessings! That is how it should go on.

There is an application to marriage too. As has been said previously, there is probably no such thing as love at first sight, although there is certainly attraction at first sight. Many couples can talk about how they first met and the feelings that they had for one another even then. Some, of course, knew each other for many years before any serious thoughts of marriage. Every couple has its own story.

My own wife grew up in Aberystwyth, where I came as a student and got to know the family. Later on, following her years at Bangor University, we met again and I decided to write and ask her out. I arranged to meet her at an evening meeting in a Christian conference she was attending to let me know if she was keen or not. She was! I can never forget the walk from the meeting to her home afterwards. My legs felt like jelly! As I was living in London and she in Aberystwyth, courting was not easy, but four months later we were engaged and soon married. I particularly recall sitting on the beach one day discussing ideals for marriage and being so pleased at how much we agreed. Over fifteen years and five children later, it is good to remember such things.

It can be interesting to ask a couple you know well, your parents for example, how they got together. It is surely good in general to keep in mind how it all began. Marriages can hit difficulties and sometimes a good antidote to troubles is to remind yourself of what attracted you to your spouse in the first place. The words are a little sentimental, but Karen Clodfelder is on the right lines:

As we grow older together,
As we continue to change with age,
There is one thing that will never change...
I will always keep falling in love with you.

Of course, some marriages get off to a shaky or unhelpful start and it is best in some ways not to dwell on how things began, although God turns situations around remarkably at times, even when they may seem hopeless. It is to such turning points that attention must then be directed.

We spoke of mothers and sons-in-law in the last chapter. This verse raises the matter of mothers and daughters-in-law, with the words, **'there your mother conceived you, there she who was in labour gave you birth'**. The man's mother gave him life and did so much more for him, but it is the beloved who rouses him now and who gives him more than his mother ever could. The transition can be problematic for some mothers-in-law as they give up their sons to another's care, but with sensitivity and wisdom on both sides there will be little difficulty. I remember how considerate my own mother was in this area. We read of Isaac and how he was comforted by his marriage to Rebekah following the death of his mother (Gen. 24:67). Here is a pattern for us to reflect on.

2. Nurture it with the right desires

In 8:6-7 it is generally agreed that it is the bride speaking. She sums up the Song's whole theme and brings it to a climax:

> **Place me like a seal over your heart,**
>   **like a seal on your arm;**
> **for love is as strong as death,**
>   **its jealousy unyielding as the grave.**
> **It burns like blazing fire,**
>   **like a mighty flame.**
> **Many waters cannot quench love;**
>   **rivers cannot wash it away.**
> **If one were to give**
>   **all the wealth of his house for love,**
>   **it would be utterly scorned.**

These words are for Longman 'arguably the most memorable and intense of the entire book'. What we have here is an earnest request to the lover, prompted by a realization of the nature of true love.

The earnest request comes first. **'Place me like a seal over your heart, like a seal on your arm,'** she begs him. In ancient times seals were used by important people, especially kings, as a relatively quick and easy, yet unique, means of identifying their authorship and ownership. By means of a ring or a pattern engraved on a pendant or bracelet, or sometimes a cylinder, a seal could be impressed in wax, so marking ownership. There is also some evidence that lovers would exchange seals.

Owen and others refer to the way the high priest wore a breastplate of precious gems over his heart and jewels on his shoulders, all sealed with the names of the tribes of Israel, and they suggest that is what is alluded to here. She is saying, according to Owen, 'Let me have an engraving, a mighty impression of love, upon thine heart, that shall never be obliterated.' Her prayer, then, is that she might belong uniquely to her lover, that she might be his alone. This is about identification, commitment and ownership. It is about being recognized, accepted and owned. She seeks an assurance that she is truly his. She wants all he is and does to reflect this.

In marriage, it is important that there should be such a pledge. Not only must the relationship be an exclusive one in terms of there not being a closer relationship with any other person, but there must also be a willingness not to let anything else so dominate one of the partners that the husband or wife is put into second place. The expression 'golf widow' is meant to be humorous, but the reality it describes may not be. To desire assurances that this is the situation is right and good.

Similarly, this is an appropriate prayer for us to address to Christ: 'Place me like a seal over your heart, like a seal on your arm.' We want every assurance that we really are his. The greater our assurance, the more certain it is, the better. Let us seek it earnestly. Meditating on the verse, John Flavel draws out the doctrine 'that there is nothing in this world which true Christians more earnestly desire than to be well assured and satisfied of the love of Jesus Christ to their souls'. He then speaks of why such an assurance is desirable and how it can be obtained. Its attraction lies in the sweetness of its enjoyment (it is the riches of faith, the rest and ease of the heart, the pleasure of life, a cordial at death and a sweet support in all troubles) and the difficulty of obtaining it (due to our own corruption, the counterfeits that exist and its grand importance). It is acquired by loving Christ more and letting him 'be much upon [our] hearts', by increasing faith in him and mourning for sin. He concludes: 'In a word; pour out thy soul to God, in hearty desires, for a sealed and clear interest in his love this day.'

3. Understand the nature of true love

The bride makes this request because she truly loves her husband. She describes her love using several images which express how strong it is. Some take this passage rather to be a description of his love to her. Perhaps we are wisest to see it as a description of true love, which will manifest itself in similar ways wherever it occurs. Many superlatives have been penned regarding love — it makes the world go round, it conquers all, it laughs at locksmiths and will always find a way. Here we have a sort of Old Testament parallel to 1 Corinthians 13.

Its strength

It is as great as that of death: **'For love is as strong as death'** (8:6). Think of the power of death. Ecclesiastes 9:1-2 speaks strikingly of it. Slowly but surely it picks us off, one by one. None can escape it. Love is as strong as that. We see it supremely in Christ and his love for his own. He even went to the point of dying on the cross in order to save them. Because he first loved us, as believers, we too ought to love him with a strong and enduring love. In marriage, husbands have the model of Christ's love for his church, and wives that of what the church ought to show to Christ.

Its intensity

It is as unyielding as the grave: **'... its jealousy unyielding as the grave'** (8:6). In Owen's words, it is as 'hard as hell'. True love is as determined as the grave itself. It is tenacious. Nothing can overthrow or defeat it. It will win out. We tend to think of jealousy as a bad thing and, of course, in fallen, sinful man it can get out of control, but jealousy itself is right and proper. True love brooks no rival. God is a jealous God, we are told (Exod. 20:5), and he will have no rivals for his people's affections. In response, we too ought to be jealous for his honour.

All this should be reflected in marriage. Woe to that person who tries to interfere with the marriage of another and arouse his or her jealousy! While we cannot condone murder, it is nevertheless true that some people have lost their lives in such a move.

Its passion

It is as unquenchable as blazing fire:

> **It burns like blazing fire,**
> **like a mighty flame.**
> **Many waters cannot quench love**
>
> (8:6).

Fire is another powerful force. No doubt you have seen film of forest fires in America, Australia or elsewhere. Despite their best efforts, firefighters cannot hold back the inferno. You may have seen at close quarters what devastation fire can cause. It is very powerful. That is what true love is like. What energy, what vigour! Do what you will to dampen it down, to quench it or quell it, still it thrives. It blazes; it flames. Even when you think it has died right down, the embers can be fanned into flame again and the blaze flares up once more.

The phrase translated **'mighty flame'** is literally 'flame of the LORD'. God is love, a great conflagration of mercy and grace. He has a passionate, unstoppable love for his own. It comes out, for example, in Hosea 11:8-9. Because he first loved us, we ought to love him too. W. W. How catches it well in the final verses of his hymn, 'It is a thing most wonderful'. Having imagined the physical agony of the cross, he says:

> But even could I see him die,
> I could but see a little part
> Of that great love, which like a fire,
> Is always burning in his heart.

> It is most wonderful to know
> His love to me so free and sure;
> But 'tis more wonderful to see
> My love for him so faint and poor.

And yet I want to love thee, Lord,
Oh, light the flame within my heart,
And I will love thee more and more,
Until I see thee as thou art.

Once again, this ought to be part of marriage too. We sometimes speak of keeping the flames of passion stoked. In marriage and in our Christian walk we must do so.

Its durability

It is as unquenchable as fire, as immovable as a rock: **'Many waters cannot quench love, rivers cannot wash it away'** (8:7). Perhaps this phrase is moving to a different picture. You know the power of water to alter the landscape. When floods come, or the sea is high, whole chunks of land can be removed and carried off. True love is not like that. It withstands such onslaughts and, like a rock in a storm, it remains unmoved despite all that may be thrown at it. Here, then, is another picture of the true love seen in Christ that ought to be reflected in our love to him and in the love that binds man and wife together in marriage.

Its preciousness

It is beyond price:

> **If one were to give
>   all the wealth of his house for love,
>   it would be utterly scorned**
>
>   (8:7).

Shakespeare has Antony say to Cleopatra, 'There's beggary in the love that can be reckoned.' It is part of the nature of true love that it cannot be bought. Sometimes people can be bought off. They want something badly, but if you get the price right they can be bribed to let it go. Every man has his price, they say. True love is not like that. If you were to say to a true lover, 'Listen, I will give you £100 if you will give up your love,' not only would he refuse you, but he would look at you with scorn. 'Okay,' you say, '£500? £1,000?' He would say to you, 'Do you understand the first thing about what real love is?' As the Beatles put it, 'Money can't buy me love.' This explains why a wife will stay with her husband even though he is poor, even though there may be many disadvantages in staying. It explains why neither bribery nor persecution can normally persuade the true believer to deny his Lord.

These images underline not only the strength of love but the danger associated with it too. Death has its sting, the grave its power to steal. Fire burns, rocks can hurt and fortunes can be squandered. What care we need to take in this whole area!

'All you need is love' was John Lennon's famous phrase. Poetically speaking, he was right, of course. However, we must understand what love is all about. Until we do, repeating the phrase, 'All you need is love', is like chanting a mere mantra. It means no more than 'Abracadabra' or 'Rhubarb, rhubarb'.

How to commence a loving covenant relationship

At this point the 'chorus' comes in again with words in the form of a question and an answer that at first sight seems rather strange and misplaced:

We have a young sister,
and her breasts are not yet grown.

What shall we do for our sister
    for the day she is spoken for?
If she is a wall,
    we will build towers of silver on her.
If she is a door,
    we will enclose her with panels of cedar
(8:8-9).

Who exactly is speaking here is debatable, but it leads us to the subject of how a covenant relationship of love begins. There are two things to note.

1. The responsibility of parents and guardians

We must note the need to be discerning. The friends seem to be recalling something the bride had told them. She would often quote the words of her brothers when she was younger. They, it seems, had brought her up. She was, presumably, orphaned at some point. **'We have a young sister,'** they would say in those days, **'and her breasts are not yet grown. What shall we do for our sister for the day she is spoken for?'**

Even though she was still young at the time, the brothers were aware of their responsibility to find a husband for her. Cultures differ, of course, and perhaps if you are a Westerner reading this and you are responsible for bringing up a little girl (or boy for that matter) you might be slow to think it your responsibility to arrange a marriage for her (or him). However, surely it is part of the responsibility of whoever brings up children to see that they are properly prepared for possible marriage. We may not go to the extent of arranging a marriage, as they do in some cultures, but there is a responsibility to bring up children to be marriageable, to endeavour to train them to be the sort of people that others will find attractive and good company, in the best sense of the terms.

Much as it may horrify the politically correct, we should teach girls to be submissive and boys to be loving and tender; we should delicately and appropriately teach children something about the facts of life (as they were once called); we should help them as best we can to meet the right sort of prospective husband or wife, and so on. Alongside appropriate teaching we must set them a good example of how to conduct oneself in the marriage relationship. It may be the Lord's will that the child we are bringing up remains single, but we do not know that and, without putting pressure on them, we should take it that our children will probably marry one day.

Of course, there is, if anything, an even greater responsibility to see that children under our care come to trust in the Lord — that they are married to him, as it were. The obligation extends beyond our own children to any we know who, like children, are ignorant and vulnerable and likely to go astray. Especially while they are still young, we must be thinking of how we can lead people to Christ wherever we can. The scope for useful work through Sunday schools, Bible clubs and similar efforts is vast.

Parents and guardians must see the need to act. It seems that there was some discussion among the brothers about how they should deal with this matter, and we may want to debate things such as what we tell children when, and what other steps we take to help them in this area. However, the idea of simply leaving it to work itself out is surely wrong. One thing the brothers were clear on was this:

> **If she is a wall,**
> **we will build towers of silver on her.**
> **If she is a door,**
> **we will enclose her with panels of cedar**
>
> (8:9).

At least one modern commentator argues that the door and the wall have the same significance. A contrast is much more likely. A door is an obvious symbol of openness, in this context openness to sexual activity, what we often refer to as promiscuity. A wall, on the other hand, is the opposite. It is closed up, not open to the idea of premarital sex, or anything approaching that. So, if she tends to be shy and chaste, modest and restrained in her dealings with boys, then we can encourage her to show herself off to best advantage, and all will be well. If, on the other hand, she proves to have a tendency to be immoral, if she is a bit of a flirt, a flibberti-gibbet, 'no better than she should be', as some might put it — then we shall have to take steps to protect her from being taken advantage of. Our actions will be like cedar — tough but not lacking sweetness.

Girls differ in their personalities and it is incumbent on parents or guardians to get to know the children they are responsible for, so that they can steer them in the right direction.

> 'Dad, I've been invited to Jason's party and it doesn't finish until midnight. Can I go?'
>
> 'Mum, can I go to the ball?'
>
> 'Is it okay for me to go and do some studying at Darren's house?'

One would presume that those bringing up young girls will want to answer such questions in different ways depending not only on how old the child is, but also on her personality. Similar applications can be made in the case of young boys, who need just as much to be encouraged or restrained according to age and character.

Once more, the same thing applies in the spiritual realm. For various reasons some are more drawn to false religions and philosophies than others. We are all different and we all struggle with different sins. Where we have responsibility towards others we must therefore take great care that no one is led astray. Think, for example, of what books you might or might not recommend to different people. Just because *you* can read something without apparent harm does not mean that everyone can.

2. Face your own growing responsibility in this matter

The sort of response one would seek from a mature young girl is the one that we find in verse 10: **'I am a wall, and my breasts are like towers.'**

She takes the idea of a **'wall'** and develops the thought. She uses a different word for 'tower' from theirs (as in 4:4; 7:4), one that emphasizes grandeur rather than defence. She says, 'Even though I'm now fast becoming a mature young woman, I'm determined to be chaste and virtuous. I know how attractive some find me, but I'm a virgin and I intend to remain one until the day I marry. It's not that I'm uninterested in boys. Rather it's that I'm determined to wait until I marry before I become intimate with a man.' By this means a young woman can win the heart of a lover such as the one described here: **'Thus I have become in his eyes like one bringing contentment.'**

The Hebrew phrases she uses could mean 'one bringing' or 'one receiving' contentment. Literally, she says, 'Thus I [i.e. the Shulammite] have become in his eyes [i.e. *Sholomo* or Solomon's] like one receiving / bringing *Shalom* [peace].' The word 'peace' contrasts with the rather military idea of towers. This is what happens when virgins wait until marriage. The very 'towers' that stand stout against invasion become a symbol of peace in due time (breasts speak of tenderness and affection).

I was once preaching on these verses in a church in Swansea. I made the point that young women should be *chaste.* Afterwards a young man approached me, on behalf of others, to ask if I had really said that young women should be *chased*! The problem is confined to spoken English and once I said that they should be pure or innocent my meaning was clear. It struck me, however, that it is usually the chaste who are chased, the pure who are pursued. Beyond an immediate interest, the unchaste are found not to be worth chasing, the impure not worth pursuing. Who will want you if you are ready to go off with more or less anyone who comes along? People are looking for constancy and commitment. True love is marked by such an attitude. It is a great pity when young women get it into their heads that the way to win love and favour is by being willing to sleep with a boy before marriage. The temptation presents itself in various forms, all the way from the lure of promiscuously bedding just about everyone through to the attraction of giving in to your fiancé and sleeping with him before your wedding night. Such a sin is always a mistake. The way to give a man contentment is to be willing to wait.

In 8:11-12 the woman uses a different figure to express her attitude:

Solomon had a vineyard in Baal Hamon;
   he let out his vineyard to tenants.
Each was to bring for its fruit
   a thousand shekels of silver [about 25 lbs or 11.5 kilos]

(8:11).

Then she goes on to speak of herself as a vineyard: **'But my own vineyard is mine to give'** (8:12). Literally she says, '*My* vineyard, which is *mine*, is before *me*.' Back in 1:6 she spoke of her brothers making her take care of their vineyards, thus causing her to neglect her own, that is herself. Perhaps they are the tenants referred to here.

'Baal Hamon' is near Dothan. Its significance is unclear although the word probably means 'Lord of the crowd' or 'Lord of abundance'. Certainly Solomon must have owned many vineyards. He also, of course, later had many wives and concubines, which could be relevant here (especially as there were a thousand all told). Yet despite all he had, he did not own her. Rather, she was willing to give the fruit of her vineyard (her affections, her time, her energy) all to him: '**... the thousand shekels are for you, O Solomon.**'

She adds, '**... and two hundred** [about 5 lbs or 2.3 kilos] **are for those who tend its fruit**' (8:12). This is cryptic, but may mean that she is not suggesting that that she has no time or affection for anyone else. She will give other members of her family (those who brought her up) their due, but Solomon comes first in her life.

So, as far as marriage is concerned, young people ought to be chaste, waiting for the time when, in the Lord's will, they find the man or woman they will marry. If you are unmarried you have a vineyard, as it were, that is yours to give. Do not give it away until the time is right. Keep it until it is time to marry.

Similarly, on the vertical plane, do not throw your life away on empty human philosophy. Give the income from your vineyard to the Owner of the vineyard and not to anyone else, except where that is due. Be devoted to him.

How to complete a loving covenant relationship

In 8:13, Solomon responds warmly to her words as he speaks for the last time:

> **You who dwell in the gardens**
> **with friends in attendance,**
> **let me hear your voice!**

The verse is difficult. It is not clear who these **'friends in attendance'** are, although the Hebrew uses the masculine form. The same term is used back in 1:7 for the shepherds. Perhaps the point is that many people love to hear the voice of this sweet girl, but he especially loves to hear it. In 1:3 she was aware that others admired him. By now he is aware that others admire her. She has come a long way. His desire to hear her has already been expressed back in 2:14.

Again and again, from every direction, you hear it noted how essential communication is in the marriage relationship. Jay Adams notes how important it is in all human relationships, but especially 'for developing and maintaining the deep intimacy that God designed for the marriage relationship'. When couples stop speaking to, and especially when they stop listening to each other, trouble is bound to follow. Again I want to protest against too rigid an understanding of male headship. A good motto for all husbands is: 'Listen to your wife!' Say to her regularly, 'Let me hear your voice.'

On a higher plane, this is how Jesus speaks to believers. 'Let me hear your voice,' he says. 'I will do whatever you ask in my name... You may ask me for anything in my name, and I will do it' (John 14:13-14). 'Call upon me in the day of trouble; I will deliver you, and you will honour me' (Ps. 50:15). He loves to have us come to him in prayer. Remember that. He has placed us in gardens of delight (that is a picture of the church); he has given us friends to attend us (brothers and sisters in Christ), but he wants to hear our voices in prayer.

She in turn responds to him by repeating the phrase:

> **Come away, my lover,**
> **and be like a gazelle**
> **or like a young stag**
> **on the spice-laden mountains**

(8:14).

The **'mountains'** could be a reference to her breasts, but are probably better understood as representing the pleasures of intimacy in general. The verse is very like 2:17. The ending, then, is not quite what we might have expected — not the two of them together in a warm embrace, but the husband listening for the wife's voice and the wife calling to her husband to come away with her. It seems that he is not there at present but she is full of anticipation about their next encounter. She is looking forward to being with him again.

This is very realistic, then. Marriage is inevitably a series of meetings and partings, hellos and goodbyes, intimacies and leave-takings. Eventually, there is the division of death. Marriage is, as we say, 'till death us do part'. However, in Christ, even then there is a reunion to look forward to — a reunion of brotherly and sisterly togetherness for ever in heaven.

The story of John Newton, author of 'Amazing Grace', and his wife, Mary Catlett, ought to be better known. Their mothers knew each other when both were young, but John's mother died when he was seven and their pathways diverged until they met again as teenagers. John was smitten, but his godless ways were a barrier to any union. In 1748 he was eventually converted and two years later they married. Forty blissful years of marriage followed.

In December 1790 Mary died after a long illness. John was at her side. He later wrote, 'When I was sure she was gone, I took off her ring, according to her repeated injunction, and put it upon my own finger. I then kneeled down, with the servants who were in the room, and returned the Lord my unfeigned thanks for her deliverance, and her peaceful dismission.'

At her funeral he said, 'I was not supported by lively, sensible considerations, but by being enabled to realize to my mind, some great and leading truths of the Word of God. I saw, what indeed I knew before, but never till then so strongly and clearly perceived, that as a sinner, I had no right, and as a believer, I could have no reason, to complain. I considered her as a loan, which He who lent her to me had a right to resume whenever He pleased; and that as I had deserved to forfeit her every day, from the first, it became me, rather, to be thankful that she was spared to me so long...'

John lived another seventeen years. In 1793 he published two volumes of letters to Mary sent over the years, a public testimony of thanks to God 'for uniting our hearts by such tender ties, and for continuing her to me for so long'.

The Christian life on earth also has its ebb and flow. It involves our repeatedly drawing near to God until that day when Christ comes again in glory. Like Enoch, we walk with God until he takes us to be with him. When that day comes we shall be with him for ever and ever and there will be no parting. As the hymn writer puts it:

In a love which cannot cease,
I am his and he is mine for ever.

As with the neighbouring books of Ecclesiastes and Proverbs, then, the Song of Songs closes with a reference to the end. We can almost hear an echo of the closing words of the Bible: 'He who testifies to these things says, "Yes, I am coming soon." Amen. Come, Lord Jesus. The grace of the Lord Jesus be with God's people. Amen' (Rev. 22:20-21).

To sum up

Marriages can hit problems — especially when there is no progress, no togetherness, or when husbands fail to shoulder their responsibilities. In difficult days sometimes the best antidote is to remind yourself of how it all began. Never forget your exclusive pledge to one another. Keep listening to each other, too.

Marriage is inevitably a series of meetings and partings, with the eventual division of death. However, in Christ there is a reunion to look forward to in heaven.

As for the rising generation, parents and guardians must recognize their responsibility and young people theirs. An unmarried person has a vineyard, as it were, that is his or hers to give. It must be kept until it is time to marry. We also have a responsibility to see that young people come to know Christ. We must be careful to lead none astray. We are responsible not to throw away our lives on empty human philosophy, but to be devoted to Christ.

On the spiritual plane, is Christ leading you out of the desert? Are you with him, leaning ever more heavily on him? How excited we were to discover Christ, how eager to receive his blessings! That is how it should go on. Pray, 'Place me like a seal over your heart, like a seal on your arm.' Seek every assurance that you are his. Because he first loved us, we ought to love him too with strong, enduring love. His passionate, unstoppable love for his own brooks no rivals and we, in return, ought to be jealous for his honour.

Appendix
Historical exposition
of the Song of Songs

Several of the Church Fathers commented on the Song, including Ambrose, Athanasius, Augustine, Chrysostom, Gregory of Nyssa, Hippolytus, Jerome, Origen (in ten volumes!) and Theoderet. It became very popular in the Middle Ages. The Venerable Bede, Gregory the Great, John of the Cross and Theresa of Avila (to the horror of her confessor, who thought it indecent for a woman to write about the Song) all tackled it. Bernard of Clairvaux and then Gilbert of Hoyland preached a total of 144 sermons from it (averaging about three sermons a verse) without reaching the end.

In the Reformation period, Martin Luther lectured on it and, although it was one of the few books for which John Calvin wrote no commentary, his successor Theodore Beza dealt with it. The Puritans were very keen on the Song. Ainsworth, Brightman, Cotton, Davenport, Durham, Hildersham, Leigh, Trapp and others wrote commentaries. The Evangelical Library in London has a fascinating volume by John Collinges (1623-1690) containing a large number of lecture-sermons on just the first two chapters. Both John Owen and Richard Sibbes (chiefly in *Bowels Opened*) commented extensively on certain chapters. A recent biography of

Samuel Rutherford explains his erotic language by the fact
that he was 'steeped in ... the Canticles' and so 'could hardly
avoid marital imagery'.

In the eighteenth century, John Gill preached 122 sermons
on the Song of Solomon. Jonathan Edwards fell in love with
the book as a teenager, finding 'an inward sweetness' in it
that sent him into raptures. He often turned to it.

In the nineteenth century, Burrowes, Hawker and Heng-
stenberg all wrote lengthy commentaries. C. H. Spurgeon
preached over sixty sermons on it. F. W. Krummacher
preached and published a series of fifteen sermons. Hudson
Taylor produced a brief devotional commentary.

Commentaries and sermons continue apace today.

No book, it seems, has had a greater diversity of interpretation. At the Westminster Assembly in the 1640s it was
observed that the 500 or so commentaries then available had
served only to increase the cloud of obscurity rather than
removing it. G. Lloyd Carr noted how in 1977, in the *Anchor
Bible Commentary*, M. H. Pope described his own 140 pages
on the problem as being primarily a 'brief sketch based on
previous summaries'!

Varied interpretation of the Song

We shall list here some of the schools of interpretation down
the years in terms of their general approach to the work.

1. Allegory, Jewish or Christian

According to this view, the Song represents either the love
between God and his ancient people, Israel, as in the Jewish
Talmuds and Targums, or the love between Christ and his
church. Such views have long been popular, fuelled in part, it
appears, by an over-fastidious desire to escape the book's

frank, though never lewd or obscene, approach to sexuality. The view is reflected in the headings given by the translators of the Authorized Version: 'The mutual love of Christ and his church' (chs. 1-3); 'The graces of the church' (ch. 4); 'Christ's love to the church' (ch. 5); 'The church professeth her faith and desire' (chs. 6-7); 'The church's love to Christ' (ch. 8).

Those who take this kind of approach disagree widely on the details, and the uncertainty about what is intended is its Achilles' heel. Another major problem is that the text never purports to be allegorical. Professor John Murray warned against 'the arbitrary and fanciful interpretations to which the allegorical view leads and which it would demand'.

2. Type

Since at least the twelfth century people have argued that the book is to be taken literally but also has a typological meaning. Many are drawn to this view, which has some similarities with the allegorical approach. A variety of suggestions are made as to the typical significance of the characters. Is the beloved Wisdom, as in Proverbs, the remnant of God's people, or even the Virgin Mary? Some note how the New Testament writer of the Epistle to the Hebrews uses Psalm 45 and argue by analogy for a similar use of the Song. It is not difficult to establish that the historical character Solomon is typical of Christ, but to take this particular book as a type creates almost as many problems as the allegorical method.

Here we note also the view of Cocceius. In 1665 he wrote of it as prophetic of church history, the culminating event being the Reformation. More recently Charles D. Alexander held that chapters 1-4 describe Old Testament religion, followed by Christ's first coming (5:1) and the anticipation of his second coming in 8:14. Such ideas echo views found in the Jewish Chaldee Targum, which makes the Babylonian exile the axis, with the book's two halves hinging on this.

3. Drama

Both in the early church and more recently, suggestions have been made that the book contains words to be acted. Origen saw it as an epithalamium, or wedding song in dramatic form. Some say it presents the love story of Solomon and the Shulammite as a drama. Others see more complexity. The Shulammite, they say, resists Solomon's advances in favour of her shepherd lover. William Still and other evangelicals accept this view.

Among other snags, the view that there are three main protagonists hits trouble when it tries to assign the masculine speeches to the two male characters posited. Quite apart from a lack of evidence for drama among the Hebrews, there are many difficulties with this view, including a lack of stage directions, long speeches and a plot that lacks a dramatic climax or resolution. Garrett says that we cannot understand it if we fail to see 'that it is lyric poetry and not drama'. With a note of authority, Carr says that, as it stands, it is 'un-actable' and 'would fail as drama'.

4. A collection of wedding songs

In the Near East there is a tradition of singing a *wasf* (an Arabic word meaning 'description' that is used as a technical term by scholars) in connection with a marriage ceremony. There are parallels between these and the Song, parallels first highlighted in the nineteenth century by Wetzstein, a German diplomat working in the Middle East. Some even want to say that the whole Song is a *wasf*.

Presented in various forms, it is an attractive view in some ways, but on closer inspection is seen to be built on shaky foundations. Significantly, the Song never speaks of the woman as queen. The idea that this is a collection of disconnected love songs is highly questionable, as the Song has a strong inner cohesion.

5. *The adaptation of a pagan liturgy*

Some scholars find here a reworking of a fertility ritual previously used in the Tammuz-Ishtar or Baal-Anath cultus or the *Marzeah* festival. Such views demand unwarranted manoeuvring of the text as it currently stands and the introduction of a number of extraneous items.

6. *A harem scene.*

Another writer sets the scene in the harem in the palace at Jerusalem. The speakers are Solomon, the girl and the harem collectively. Some rearrangement of the material is again involved. Surely this is a non-starter.

7. *Political*

Another writer sees the book in terms of post-exilic politics. There is evidence that Luther too favoured a political approach, but nothing in the text supports such a view.

An outline of the Song's construction

The book is difficult to analyse, but *inclusios* in 1:4 and 8:14 ('Take me away' / 'Come away') point to a careful structure centring on 4:16 and 5:1 and the exchange: 'Let my lover come into his garden... I have come into my garden.' There are also four sets of repeated refrains:

1. 'Daughters of Jerusalem, I charge you' (2:7; 3:5; 5:8; 8:4).

2. 'My lover is mine and I am his', or variants on this (2:16; 6:3; 7:10).

3. 'His left arm is under my head...' (2:6: 8:3).

4. 'Like a gazelle or a young stag...' (2:9,17; 8:14).

There are also clear parallels (e.g., 3:1-5 with 5:2-8; 4:1-7 with 6:4-10; 2:8-13 with 7:12-13). Some discover a chiastic, even concentric, arrangement in the book, which seems likely.

In the first chapter we explained Glickman's approach. Slightly different is that of Carr and R. K. Harrison, who posit five and six sections respectively. Carr sees a pattern of invitation, exhilaration and warning. The end of each section is indicated by the repeated use of 'Do not arouse or awaken love until ...' (2:7; 3:5; 8:4), with what he describes as 'consummation terminators' at the end of 5:1 and in 8:14.

He also sees a pattern in the way that the sections begin and so has the following structure:

1:1 – 2:7	Anticipation	Bride longs for groom
2:8 – 3:5	Found and lost – and found	Increasing love; maiden's praise
3:6 – 5:1	Consummation	King's praise; espousal; bride's praise
5:2 – 8:4	Lost – and found	Bride longs for groom; her beauty described
8:5-14	Affirmation	Conclusion: the durability of true love

An attractive fourfold division of the book appears in a chart produced by American publisher Thomas Nelson:

1:1 – 5:1 The beginning of love

1:1 – 3:5	Falling in love	Courtship — the fostering of love
3:6 – 5:1	United in love	Wedding — the fulfilment of love

5:2 – 8:14 The broadening of love

5:2 – 7:10	Struggling in love	Problem — the frustration of love
7:11 – 8:14	Growing in love	Progress — the faithfulness of love

Linguistic expression in the Song

Although the book has only 117 verses, they contain a surprisingly large number of unusual words. According to Carr, some forty-seven, out of a total of 470 different Hebrew words used, are exclusive to the Song. Of those that do appear elsewhere in the Old Testament, over 120 are 'unusual' or 'fairly unusual'. The other 300 or so can be thought of as 'common'. This means that sometimes it is difficult to establish the exact meaning of words due to a lack of clear context.

Much of the vocabulary is typical of love poetry. The lovers meet in gardens, fields, orchards or vineyards. There are many references to flora and fauna. One authority says that fifteen species of animal and twenty-one varieties of plant are mentioned. There are also fitting references to jewellery, precious stones, gold, fruit, honey, spices and perfumes. There is plenty of local colour, stemming from the particular flora and fauna and the place names used.

Like the book of Esther, the Song is distinguished by a striking failure to make any direct reference to God. In fact, for a book in the Bible, it is remarkably free from most theological or religious terms. This may account for why it appears never to be quoted in the New Testament. It also perhaps underlines the importance of understanding the book first of all in natural terms.

Select bibliography

The main commentaries consulted in preparing this present commentary (in chronological order of publication) are listed below.

The [sv] and [nh] notations indicate whether the commentary takes a chiefly spiritual / vertical or natural / horizontal view.

Durham, James. *Exposition of the Song of Songs* (1669), Banner of Truth edition [sv]

Henry, Matthew. *Commentary on the Whole Bible* (1710), MacDonald edition [sv]

Burrowes, George. *A Commentary on Song of Songs* (1853), Banner of Truth edition [sv]

Robinson, Thomas. *The Preachers' Homiletical Commentary* (1891), Baker edition [sv]

Glickman, S. Craig. *A Song for Lovers* (1976), Intervarsity Press, USA [nh]

Carr, G. Lloyd. *The Song of Solomon* (1984), IVP Tyndale Old Testament Commentary series (General editor: D. J. Wiseman) [nh]

Garrett, Duane A. *Proverbs, Ecclesiastes, Song of Songs* (1993), The New American Commentary, Broadman Press [nh]

Gledhill, Tom. *The Message of Song of Songs* (1994), IVP Bible Speaks Today series (Old Testament Editor: J. A. Motyer) [nh]

Brooks, Richard. *Song of Solomon* (1999), Focus on the Bible series, Christian Focus Publications [sv]

Huwiler, Elizabeth. *Proverbs, Ecclesiastes, Song of Songs* (1999), New International Bible Commentary (Old Testament Editors: R. L. Hubbard, R. K. Johnston) [nh]

Longman III, Tremper. *Song of Songs* (2001), The New International Commentary on the Old Testament (General Editor: Robert L Hubbard) [nh]

Masters, Peter. *The Mutual Love of Christ and his People* (2004), Wakeman Press [sv]

Among other volumes consulted were Barry Webb's *Five Festal Garments* [nh], relevant parts of Richard Sibbes' *Works* [sv], volume 2 of John Owen's *Works* [sv], and the summary of his thought on the Song of Solomon in Sinclair Ferguson's *John Owen on the Christian Life*, pp. 77-85. Help was also obtained from a sermon series by Derek Thomas in Jackson, Mississippi, available online [nh].